DOING DI|

Politics and the Labour Movement in Norwich

1880-1914

CEAS

Steven Cherry

Front cover: *'Dinnertime' : men leaving Carrow works, c.1905*

Back cover: *Independent Labour Party Voting Card, Norwich Municipal Election 1904 (by kind permission of the Local Studies Department, Norwich Central Library).*

Cover Design by Richard Malt
Printed by Witley Press Ltd., Hunstanton, England.

ISBN 0-906219 26 4
©Centre of East Anglian Studies 1989

Centre of East Anglian Studies
University of East Anglia
Norwich NR4 7TJ.

Contents

Photographs

Acknowledgements

The Labour Movement in Norwich has been rather neglected as a subject of local history and overlooked by otherwise comprehensive national accounts of labour history. If this study helps to remedy either of these deficiences I shall be well pleased.

In any event, I am grateful to many people. The staff at the Local Studies Department of the Norwich Central Library and colleagues in the Economic and Social History sector at the University of East Anglia have displayed differing forms of patience with my endeavours in producing this book. I wish also to acknowledge the generosity of Mr Tony Rogers of Merthyr Tydfil, Colman Foods and the Norwich Central Library Local Studies Department in allowing me to use the photographs which appear respectively on page 19, the front cover, page 93, and the back cover. I thank Mavis Bithray of the Centre of East Anglian Studies who typed several drafts of everything else that appears between the covers and Barry Doyle who converted the original photographs into a reproducable form and provided additional information on them.

I owe especial debts to Gerald Crompton, for stimulating my interest in labour history and to Richard Wilson, who ensured that I completed this contribution in a readable and hopefully coherent form. Equally I am grateful to Hassell Smith, Director of the Centre of East Anglian Studies at UEA, for a great deal of practical assistance and a willingness to publish in what is for the Centre a new area. Financial support was also kindly provided by the School of Economic and Social Studies at UEA, the Norwich and District Trades Union Council and its affiliated branches, particularly the MSF Norwich 246 branch, and by my fellow members of Norwich SWP. Hopefully, all will consider this book a worthwhile result for their respective efforts and none bear responsibility for my own interpretations or shortcomings.

Finally, I want to thank my most supportive critic, Joan, and our young but patient daughters, Frances and Helen. For as long as all three have known me I have been attempting to produce this book, and so to them it is dedicated.

1

Introduction

Background

Noting that Norwich was to be the venue for the 1894 Trades Union Congress the new *Labour Leader* newspaper commented,

> In this bare announcement what possibilities are concealed? Norwich, the centre of 'Dumpling Land', and one of the homes of non-union labour is to be invaded by the Trades Union agitator.[1]

There was evidence to justify at least in part this unflattering view. In the General Elections of 1885 and 1892 the city, or rather the minority which had the vote, returned as its MPs the 'Mustard Millionaire', J.J. Colman (Liberal) and the county banker, Sir Samuel Hoare (Conservative). As yet there was no branch of the Independent Labour Party, and the local Trades Council, which had existed for eight years, was weak and under the political influence of the Liberals.

On the other hand, Norwich had already experienced the rise and extension of trade union activity associated with the 'New Unionism' in the late 1880s and had seen a strike wave of sorts in 1890-1. Prior to this there had been radical and socialist agitations of unexpectedly large proportions. The local branch of the Socialist League had more than 150 members in 1887,[2] and 'advanced radical' elements within the Liberal Party had been able to secure the election of an 'independent socialist' against the sitting Liberal councillor in the municipal contests of 1886. Similarly there was a radical tradition, including trade unionism as well as Primitive Methodism, in the surrounding countryside which was not extinguished, despite the severe reverses suffered by Norfolk farmworkers in the early 1890s.[3] Thus, if the *Labour Leader*'s assessment of Norwich seemed apt in 1894, it understated the fluctuating experiences of the Norwich Labour Movement over the preceding decade.

These were to continue. In the early 1900s Norwich became one of the few places outside Yorkshire and Lancashire where the ILP established a strong base, and was among the first cities to elect a Labour MP, G.H. Roberts, in 1906. By 1910 Norwich ILP had a membership, on paper at least, of 800, and it was the party to which five of the six Labour councillors and most of the eight Labour Poor Law Guardians belonged in 1913. Yet wage rates, the proportion of trade unionists, and the level of strikes in Norwich remained among the lowest in the country even in these years. Moreover, the great wave of industrial unrest in Britain and Ireland between 1909 and 1913 caused hardly a ripple in the city.

To explain the nature of the Labour Movement in Norwich is therefore not likely to be easy. Apart from individual trade union or industrial histories which have a direct connection with the city, only a handful of published accounts provide brief references.[4] The detailed survey of social conditions compiled by C.B. Hawkins before 1910 has no parallel in the Labour Movement as such, though recent research has thrown more light upon the Norfolk farmworkers, and upon the Norwich Labour Party and its relations with Liberalism.[5]

Among the more obvious reasons for this lack of information on the Labour Movement before 1914 are the problems associated with source materials and some alleged characteristics of the movement itself. In addition to the main local newspapers there was a radical weekly, *Daylight*, which for most of the period 1878-1902 regularly provided comment upon trade union and local political developments, though the presentation of this information was subjected to the whims of its erratic owner, Edmund Burgess. Nominally a Liberal, he was at various times sympathetic to the Socialist League and the ILP, though out of touch with organised Labour by the early 1900s. Three other newspapers, all short-lived, were Liberal influenced and targeted at trade unionists in Norwich and Norfolk in the 1890s, while in the early 1900s equally temporary papers espoused the causes of municipalisation and Labour Representation.[6] Each of these provides sufficient material to compose a series of snapshots, at least, of the local Labour Movement and there is no shortage of relevant electoral material.[7]

While allowance must be made for the respective political interpretations inherent in these sources, problems arise from the selection, or more usually exclusion, of information. Much press coverage was refracted through local journalists or editors with the result that the ideas and even the names of many local activists, excepting a number of leading or known personalities, are lost. Similarly the desire to present local or topical aspects might devalue the level of awareness of national issues or historical understanding which these activists really possessed. The search for good copy, or what were deemed the important angles, excluded much of the routine but typical features of trade unionism and virtually obliterated, for example, the role of women in the unions or political organisations. What remains is largely a record of disputes, electoral contests, and episodes in the life of political groups or parties. This is valuable but less than comprehensive, and all that can be done is to proceed, utilising available detail, in the knowledge that such difficulties with source materials are neither insurmountable nor confined to the Labour Movement.

Some supposed characteristics of the local Labour Movement may also stem from the problems outlined. Norwich cannot be seen as a storm centre of labour militancy and the local emphasis on 'doing different' sometimes meant doing badly in the context of trade union organisation. But this alleged tradition did not necessarily govern the ideas and responses of Norwich workers, nor did it stem from a purely parochial standpoint. To treat Norwich simply as an uninteresting and unchanging Labour backwater misses the opportunity to examine features that were not always atypical of the Labour Movement generally in the late nineteenth and early twentieth centuries. An often isolated and weak trade unionism which nevertheless had its moments, the durability of Liberalism in some sections of the working class, and the transition from active to more passive aspects in the socialism of others are features whose interconnections are worth exploring. They are also not likely to be unique to Norwich.[8] Interlinked with this, the difficulties of assessing the relative impact of specifically 'local' or 'national' aspects of Labour Movement activity, for example in voting patterns in General Elections, pose special problems. Yet these may also offer rewards if the Norwich experiences can shed further light upon current controversies among historians, not least the question of whether a revived New Liberalism had 'contained' the rise of Labour by 1914.

It is impossible to detail all the processes whereby differing political ideas were taken up within the Norwich Labour Movement, but interpretations which rely only upon the class position of workers inevitably propelling them towards Labour Representation, or those which seek to define the politics of Labour solely in terms of responses to New Liberalism, are unsatisfactory.[9] Making due allowance for the effects of the industrial structure, the state of the economy and geographical features upon the Labour Movement, the emphasis is still upon the ideas and activities within the movement, which were not fully encapsulated in the conflict between Liberal and Labour. From roughly 1880 to 1914 socialists, radicals and trade unionists in Norwich variously attempted to make converts to Revolutionary Socialism, to build and consolidate trade unionism, to permeate the Liberal Party with the approaches of collectivism and municipalisation, and to establish new parties capable of winning local and Parliamentary elections. In developing these strategies workers in Norwich were emulating other workers, often in much bigger industrial centres, and they were subjected to pressures from outside their direct experience in terms of class and area. Local practices and whether these can be explained in terms other than the cliché that Norfolk always tends to 'do different' can hopefully be highlighted within the context of a general historical account.

Economic and Occupational Structure

The conditions which faced the local working population in the decades before and after 1900 hardly favoured Labour organisation. Between 1881 and 1911 the population of Norwich expanded by 38%, from 87,842 to 121,478, and much of this increase reflected the flow of ex-agricultural labourers and their families from the depressed Norfolk countryside. The population of Norfolk, excluding Norwich, rose by a mere 4% between 1881 and 1911, while in the 1890s alone the number of farm labourers in Norfolk fell by 5,500 or 14%.[10] The very isolation of Norwich from other industrial centres contributed to the build-up of labour in the city, a feature stressed by trade unionists and social commentators alike: 'Once a man finds himself in Norwich he cannot easily get out of it. He is not wanted in the county, and if he were he would probably find a difficulty in securing house room for his family, and even a single ticket to any large town will cost him from 8/- to 10/-'.[11] Relative isolation was also likely to be a retarding factor in the spread of new ideas in the Labour Movement. While political speakers, trade union activists and newspapers travelled easily enough, national issues tended to be seen by local workers mainly in terms of their own narrower experiences. Even had other features in

Norwich been favourable, those outlined so far were likely to have a downward pressure on wage levels and dilute any 'knock-on' effects of trade union militancy in other towns and cities.

Neither the local industrial structure nor the nature of the labour market helped labour organisation. Norwich lacked those heavy, large-scale industries in which workers might be concentrated. Correspondingly the sizeable sections of skilled workers in a strong bargaining position, containing the core of trade union activists, were also missing. In the period under discussion the city's major industries were boot and shoemaking, which employed 15% of male workers, and building, transport, and food and drink processing, which each employed a further 10%.[12] Other significant occupational groupings between 1881 and 1911 were 'general labour', employing 6% of working males, woodworking and furnishings (4%), agriculture (4%), printing and paper, textiles, tailoring, and domestic service, (each employing 2%). Workers in the four major industries were rarely concentrated together in large numbers, and the work in them was often very irregular. The building industry was characteristically diverse and subject to cyclical and seasonal fluctuations. Railway work was more regular but not markedly concentrated and it comprised only a quarter of the occupations listed under 'transport' in the area. Many of the others, especially carting, portering and stowage, were scattered and irregular, particularly in a city which, as a marketing centre for agricultural Norfolk, had proportionately large livestock and vegetable markets and any number of attendant, brief, odd jobs. Parts of the food and drink processing industries were becoming increasingly mechanised, employing a factory labour force, but a noted example, Colmans, remained the exception not the rule. Other large employers, such as Caleys, the sweet and chocolate concern, continued to rely upon a version of the putting-out system, with the bulk of packaging, wrapping etc. being carried out on an off-site basis. If the brewing industry provided regular work, breweries were not traditionally large employers of labour, in spite of their growing scale. Food and drink processing was often subject to seasonal fluctuation, which affected the numbers of workers employed, and the distribution and retailing sides of this sector remained small-scale and scattered.

The exception to all this may well have been the boot and shoe industry, as technological change and the resultant factory mode of production had contributed to the emergence of just five large firms, with Howlett and

White, Southalls, Haldensteins, Edwards and Holmes, and Sextons employing almost half the 7,800 men who gave their occupation as boot or shoeworker in the 1901 and 1911 Census Returns. But even here there were no less than seventy-three other factory or workshop producers as late as 1896, and a considerable amount of outworking was conducted on a regular basis until well into the 1900s.[13]

For women workers these problems were even more marked. There was a pronounced sexual imbalance in the Norwich population to the extent of an average ratio of women to men of 54 to 46 between 1881 and 1911. A considerable proportion of these women were in waged work. Between 38% and 42% of all women and girls aged over ten years earned wages according to the census data, with corresponding figures for women and girls aged over fifteen years fluctuating between 40% and 45%.[14] Women in Norwich comprised roughly 40% of the city labour force in 1881 and 1891, a proportion which had declined to 35% by 1911. This was higher than the national average figure of approximately 30%. Similarly the proportion of married women working between 1901 and 1911, 17% in Norwich, compared with a national average of 14% in urban areas. No less than 32% of working women in the city were in domestic service or charring, occupations in which conditions and pay were notoriously bad and virtually impossible for trade unions to organise.[15] A further 26% of the employed women had work in the textile industries, the remnants of the weaving trades or the expanding clothing industry. These were strongholds of sweated work, and vulnerable to the variabilities of season and fashion. About 13% of working women were in the boot and shoe industry, particularly in the lowest paid 'garret' sectors, while another 7% worked in the largely fragmented food and drink industry.

Where there was direct competition for work between men and women there could only be further depressing effects on wage levels. This was a feature rather over-emphasised by Hawkins as a chief cause of poverty and a problem bemoaned but not solved by trade unionists. Child labour, still extensive at the turn of the century, had similar consequences, especially in the shoe and clothing industries.[16] The basic background obstacles to workers' organisation and better wages can therefore be summarised as the city's geographic isolation, the small scale and fragmentation of some industries and the continuation of outwork and sweating in others, and the operation of that vicious circle whereby low wages necessitated more women and children working, which further perpetuated a system of overlap and competition. Added to this complex situation was the inflow of agricultural labour which encouraged the persistence of casual work. Absent from it was a 'leading group' of workers - miners or dockers for example - who might have acted as a catalyst for wider labour organisation.[17]

Just how important these background constraints themselves were would only become apparent as workers attempted to organise within them. Yet there was nothing inevitable about the extent to which trade unionism or socialist influence would be retarded by such conditions. The fact that workers in Norwich took virtually no direct part in the national explosion of industrial unrest after 1909, for example, cannot sufficiently be explained by the economic conditions cited so far. Clearly, we should examine the approaches adopted by workers as the subjects of history, and the impact upon them of other influences, such as changes in the policies of the Liberal Party, over time. Thus the attempt to examine differing strategies provides the best explanation of the development of the Labour Movement in Norwich.

Trade Unions and Political Activity up to the Middle 1880s

In the early 1870s when 'the revolt of the field' shook Norfolk, trade unionism in Norwich, a radical city by tradition, was limited and quiescent. According to the listings of industrial disputes compiled by G.P. Bevan, there had been no major strikes in the city in the 1860s.[18] The one big dispute recalled by the contemporary trade unionist, J.L. Hawkins, in the 1870s was 'the great lock-out of rivetters and finishers' which affected 600 shoe workers in 1872.[19] Even in this case the workers were not very well organised and the union involved, the Amalgamated Cordwainers Association, which became the Amalgamated Society of Boot and Shoemakers in 1873, numbered just 178 members in Norwich by February 1874. This was at a time when there were perhaps 6,000 shoe workers in and around the city, and the union's national membership was 8,300. In comparison, in shoemaking centres such as Leicester and Stafford the union had respectively 1,288 and 592 members.[20]

Other trade unions were also thin on the ground in Norwich. The

Amalgamated Society of Engineers claimed forty-four members in 1862, while the Amalgamated Society of Carpenters and Joiners had fifty-nine members in 1871, and there can have been but a sprinkling of union members in the rest of the building, printing and tailoring trades.[21] Among unskilled workers the Amalgamated Labour League and the National Agricultural Labourers Union had attempted to organise but they had little success, and both these agriculturally-based unions declined after 1873.[22]

Within the Norwich unions there were already calls for repeal of the Criminal Law Amendment Act, which restricted trade union tactics such as picketing, and for the extension of the suffrage in the 1870s. Similarly some thirty-four trade unionists had established the local Co-operative Society in 1875.[22] But trade unionism as a fighting force was very limited, and its real growth in the city was to take place in the different circumstances of the late 1880s, when socialist ideas were to play a role. At least until then Liberal ideas predominated in unions and city alike. The period under study opens with the General Election of 1880 when the city returned two Liberal MPs for the first time, though neither J.J. Colman nor J.H. Tillett could be said to represent the most radical elements within Liberalism. Alongside the Liberals an 'Independent Association', a loose grouping of radicals and ratepayers in which Edmund Burgess was prominent, enjoyed brief success in local elections in the early 1880s.

Though not immune from the crises which affected the Liberal Party nationally in the 1880s, especially the questions of further electoral reform and Home Rule in Ireland, Norwich Liberalism was also shaped by local features. On the one hand some buoyancy was obtained from rural successes in Norfolk. Here the decline of agricultural trade unionism and the extension of the vote to rural areas provided both a motive and a means for electoral activity. This was encouraged by the Norfolk County Franchise Association, which mobilised Liberal support in the unions and villages, and by the National Reform Union. The latter held a series of meetings throughout Norfolk in 1885 addressed by the veteran Manchester Chartist, W.H. Chadwick, in order 'To assist in forming district, village and town Liberal Associations' and to mobilise the new voters.[24] The connections between Norfolk farmworkers and the Liberal Party were reinforced by the attachment of both to Nonconformity and demands for secular education. Primitive Methodism was especially strong in Norfolk, where the links between the established church and the landowners and farmers

were all too obvious.[25] Thus, in the 1885 General Election those farmworkers who were enfranchised, '... trooped to the polls to vote against the
squire and parson and farmer the only way they could - by voting
Liberal'.[26] There was some understanding of class relations in this action but
it was as yet incomplete. So long as trade unionism remained weak, Liberal
demands for secular education, separation of Church and State, further
extension of the vote, and promises of land reform were likely to remain a
source of hope and a pole of attraction to Norfolk farmworkers.

To an extent this was also true in Norwich, though there were
differences within the labour orientated, radical wing of Liberalism. Some
elements here were already sceptical of the reforming ambitions of leading
local Liberal figures and the latter, if they were aware of the need to control
a large and 'loyal' working class base to bolster Liberal support at election
times, had already begun to view the development of more radical ideas
with some alarm.[27] These tensions became clearer with the growth of trade
unionism - J.J. Colman had his own battles with the Gasworkers and
General Labourers Union in the 1890s for example - but they were already
visible in the mid-1880s. For in May 1885, alongside the city's National
Liberal Federation, a new body, the Norwich Democratic Association,
began to hold public meetings. Though the timing of these coincided with
the efforts of the National Reform Union in the county, the Norwich
Democratic Association's purpose went beyond the obtaining of Liberal
votes. It contained more working class radicals than small employers and
was the forum for the handful of socialists then in Norwich. Leading figures
included Edmund Burgess, F.J. Crotch, who had a small bill-posting
business, W.T. Scarles, a Liberal trade unionist soon to be involved in setting
up the Norwich Trades Council, C. Reynolds, a socialist plasterer, and F.C.
Slaughter, about to become a key figure in the Norwich branch of the
Socialist League.

While there are parallels with the Democratic Federation of 1881-4, the
Norwich Democratic Association was not a remnant of this, nor was it
destined to become a branch of the Social Democratic Federation, though
there were one or two Social Democratic Federation members in Norwich
in 1885. At the end of May the Norwich Democratic Association initiated
a debate on the question 'Will Socialism benefit the English People?' and in
July opened a propaganda fund.[28] By September the group was in
correspondence with the Social Democratic Federation over the 'Free

Speech' fights going on in London, raising money for these, and informed the local press that they were 'also desirous of hearing at first hand from one of the recognised leaders of the movement what their views really are, and what Socialism really is'. William Morris, Edward Aveling and Henry Hyndman were identified as suitable figures and they were offered a £2 expenses fee.[29]

At this point the Norwich grouping was not formally committed to socialist objectives and in November it suspended meetings, ostensibly to enable its members to take part in electoral campaigning. But when reconstituted in December it had now become the Norwich Pioneer Class for the Discussion of Socialism, with F.C. Slaughter very much its driving force.[30] The 1885 General Election was not responsible for this change of title, which as yet affected only socialists and a small minority of radicals, but one aspect of the campaign had a much wider impact on Norwich Liberals. A feature of the election, in which the Tory brewer Henry Bullard became senior member for the city, was the systematic breaking up of Liberal meetings by 'roughs'. This kind of activity had been a regular feature of the Norwich elections but its scale led to petitioning, upheld in court on 3 April 1886, that the election result be made void. The judges decided that there had been 'corrupt practices' by Bullard's election agents, which was putting the matter delicately. In the trial it emerged that a considerable number of men, frequently employees of Bullard's Brewery, were paid between 1/- and 2/6d per session to break up Liberal meetings. There had also been an abnormally high number of 'free beer treats' for roughs and electors, particularly at Bullard's tied public houses. Similarly, considerable, undeclared Conservative expenses had been used to sustain the print run of the Tory *Norfolk Standard* at roughly six times its normal level for the duration of the campaign.[31]

Yet when a writ was issued for a new election the local Liberal leadership, which had not organised the petitioning, declined to field a candidate. Apparently honour was satisfied and the Tory banker Sir Samuel Hoare, who thus gained an uncontested seat, was an acceptable replacement for Bullard. Those radicals who had initiated the petitioning were not enthralled with the prospect of Hoare as one of their representatives, especially when the second Norwich seat was now arguably within the Liberals' grasp, and were furious at the conduct of the senior Liberal figures. But as *Daylight*, by now the voice of the radicals, commented, 'The great body of Radical electors may protest and fume and fret; their masters know their bark is worse than their bite'.[32] The paper went on to argue that the radicals would be treated in this fashion until they could organise and build up their own election funds, thereby achieving independence from the Liberal 'wire pullers'.

Such comments did not imply separate and independent Labour representation, nor had they a wide following, but this early public airing of radical discontent within the Liberal Party was soon followed by an act of defiance. In the municipal elections of November 1886 Liberals in the Eighth ward selected F.J. Crotch, a former member of the Norwich Democratic Association who now described himself as an 'independent socialist', to run against the sitting Liberal member, J. Hunter, the leader of the Liberal group on the city council. Crotch and a second Liberal, Ladell, polled 412 and 414 votes respectively, leaving Hunter unelected in third place.[33] This successful assertion of independence, albeit limited in extent, suggested that radical interests might be advanced within the Liberal Party, and other 'working-men rads' were adopted as official Liberal candidates in municipal elections within a few years. Over the 1890s J. Mason, J. Williment and W.E. Scarlett were regularly re-elected as Liberal councillors on this basis.[34] Yet this result did not indicate the emergence of independent Labour representation or the successful permeation of the Liberal Party with socialist ideas. Rather, it revealed that the local Liberal leadership knew when to be amenable to pressure from the Liberal base. Liberal leaders could appreciate the electoral value of 'safe' candidates and the containing effect of the selection of local working-men radical candidates. Such awareness served them well as more serious forms of opposition began to develop outside, and later inside, Liberal ranks.

2

Making Socialists

The Socialist League in Norwich 1885-92

Since the Socialist League existed for less than seven years, locally and nationally, and as there is speculation as to whether its national membership even came near to one thousand, its relevance to this study might appear marginal. More perhaps might be said for the Social Democratic Federation, which at least had individual members in Norwich throughout the period 1885-1914 and which seemed capable of challenging the Independent Labour Party for the loyalties of socialist workers in the late 1890s and again, as the British Socialist Party, around 1912.[1] Both the League and the SDF emphasised that socialism was an alternative, replacement system to capitalism, and while neither precisely detailed how this transformation was to occur, each placed great stress upon making individual socialists.[2] That it should be a branch of the Socialist League which was formed in Norwich reflected the opinions of a small number of socialists rather than a great debate in the local Labour Movement. And what had become the anarchism of the Norwich branch ensured that at the time of its collapse in 1892 the organisation was again marginal.

Yet in the late 1880s the Socialist League was able to exert a major influence in the city, reviving and redirecting an anti-capitalist radicalism not seen since the days of the Chartists, with a detectable impact among many trade unionists and upon many of the socialists who sought to build a movement capable of securing Labour Representation. That such forms of labour organisation with their limited, essentially pragmatic approaches should so outlast the Socialist League with its grand visions and objectives, was, in part, its unintended and hugely ironic legacy.

The immediate origins of the Socialist League in Norwich lie not in the rupture of an existing SDF branch, as was normally the case, but as an extension of that socialist campaigning which had turned the radical

Norwich Democratic Association into the more specific Pioneer Class for the Discussion of Socialism. It was reported that on 7 February 1886, 'At the usual meeting of this class . . . the two latest manifestoes of the SDF and the Socialist League were read, and after a full discussion by the members it was unanimously agreed to join the Socialist League, as being the more advanced, and to form a Norwich branch'.[3] As few as eleven people may have been party to this decision, but the speed with which an executive committee of nine was established indicates growth, or at least its expectations, in the branch.[4] For with a layer of radical contacts from the Norwich Democratic Association days, constant publicity throughout the autumn of 1885 and the prospect of William Morris's attendance at the League's inaugural public meeting, a sound beginning was reasonably anticipated.

Morris himself described how '. . . I went to Norwich and lectured to a very good audience, some eight hundred I should think at the Victoria Hall . . . the audience was mostly working class and was or seemed to be quite in sympathy with the movement'.[5] His speech expressed an awareness of class society and argued for its elimination through socialism, but he emphasised the importance of making and educating socialists. Certainly he did not imply social transformation through class struggle. The movement for socialism he felt would meet '. . . no forcible resistance unless the upper class can delude some part of the workers to take part in defence of their unjust and pernicious position . . . I believe that if the intelligent of the working class and the honourable and generous of the employing class could learn to see the system under which we live as it really is, all the dangers of change would seem nothing to them, and our capitalistic society would not be worth six months purchase'.[6]

Though Morris was a national figure the size of his audience was no freak incident. For a few weeks the League relied on open-air meetings with pitches in the city centre and in the outlying villages of St Faith's, Costessey and Drayton. These were addressed by visiting speakers such as Morris or Frank Kitz or regulars like Charles Mowbray and Fred Henderson, both of whom had moved to Norwich.[7] All attracted sizeable crowds and by July the branch secretary, 'Fred Charles' Slaughter, reported in *The Commonweal* that 'things are moving gloriously at Norwich'.[8] Large crowds had attended open-air meetings in the city centre over the Easter weekend, and by October J.L. Mahon and Morris were heard by audiences

Norwich Branch of the Socialist League in 1885. William Morris (with stick) is seated in the centre. To his left are the young Fred Henderson and Lucy Slaughter.

respectively one and two thousand strong.[9] On 7 November Henderson addressed '. . . several thousands . . . the largest socialist meeting yet seen in Norwich', with 240 copies of *The Commonweal* sold at this and another meeting, while the League's main event in December was '. . . attended by upwards of 2,000 persons who gave three ringing cheers for the Social Revolution'.[10]

What was the attraction of the League? On his first visit to Norwich, Morris noted, 'The working class there are in a sad plight: the old weaving industries are fast perishing; the modern industry of mechanical shoe-making is hard pressed by foreign competition and the "hands" are terribly exploited'.[11] If not the most penetrating of economic analyses this pinpointed one potential area of support, the handcraft workers whose livelihood was threatened by factory industrialisation. It has been suggested in more recent times that 'The Norwich shoemakers who joined the Socialist League were, like the Chartist handloom weavers, making a protest against the harshness of the extending industrial system, which had no use for their craftsmenship'.[12] These observations overstate the number of shoeworkers likely to join the League while underplaying the wider political ideas in the heads of those who did join it. The vision of socialism offered by the Socialist League went well beyond memories of some halcyon days of craft production, and its members, if not all its audiences, looked very much forwards to socialism. Thus while there were meetings on subjects such as 'A glance at the working classes over 100 years', these were outnumbered by those on issues ranging from 'Socialism and Free Thought' or 'Christianity and Socialism' to 'The position of women today and under Socialism'.[13] Some idea of the League's basic appeal to farmworkers in the villages surrounding Norwich can be derived from the alarmist handbills produced by the Reverend Ballance, Vicar of St Faith's, where the League had established a presence: 'Beware of these men! They revile the Queen, calling her a German Pauper! They revile the clergy and landowners, calling them thieves! They say one man is as good as another and the land was meant for all. What a dreadful set . . . touch none of their papers!'[14]

The problems of being unable to affect existing standards of living and working conditions, and of recruiting and retaining members, were overlooked in the inspirational first few months. Although the size and enthusiasm of meetings would hardly be underestimated in *The Commonweal* reports, clearly the League was making considerable headway in the second half of 1886. Most obviously, the Norwich membership rose from sixty in October to eighty-eight by the end of November, and the branch had opened reading and lecture rooms in two parts of the city, St Benedicts and Ber Street.[15] From the outset Morris had been impressed by the members in Norwich, '. . . with their hearts in the business and with no thought of compromise, thoroughly understanding the futility of Parliamentary agitation'.[16] The newer recruits flung themselves into the high level of activity necessary to sustain the number of small meetings going on around Norwich, to attract crowds to major marketplace meetings and to raise the readership of *The Commonweal*.[17] Sales of the paper at public meetings varied between 20 and 240, with up to 20 papers sold regularly at village meetings in Sprowston, Drayton and St Faith's.[18] Yet the contrasts between the activity of League members, and their ability to draw crowds, and its capacity to organise wider support on a day-to-day basis in the Labour Movement were already apparent. Similarly, the enthusiasm for Socialism was not matched by knowledge of the practical steps which might be taken to move toward this goal. Rounds of meetings to 'make socialists', while initially successful, could eventually tire existing members and pose additional problems. For example, while the attempts by the vicar of St Faith's to prevent the League from establishing a presence there had actually helped it, the new St Faith's branch could not be sustained without still further effort from Norwich members. Clashes with a more organised wing of Christianity proved more serious, as members of the Salvation Army, disputing with the League over 'pitches' within the city, began to pass on the names of Socialist League members to local employers. This led to victimisations which the League was unable to prevent.[19] City authorities and landlords also combined to deny the League use of public halls during the winter of 1886-7, causing for example the cancellation of Annie Besant's speaking tour.[20]

A further reason for the growing interest in the Socialist League was the sharp cyclical rise in unemployment in 1886, which aggravated the usual problems associated in Norwich with seasonal unemployment. Denied meeting facilities and attempting to build upon the support it was attracting, the League took to the streets and began agitation among the unemployed. Again this had initial results but once more posed longer-term problems. Parades of the unemployed, called for the end of December, had to be postponed because the weather was so bad. They began on the evening of 3 January with a marketplace rally addressed by League speakers, Henderson and Mowbray, and chaired by the radical councillor Crotch. The parade took the form of a march around the city which was generally good-humoured, except when passing the premises of particularly notorious employers, such as Haldensteins' shoeworks, where 'much groaning and hooting commenced'.[21]

Such demonstrations were relatively common in Norwich and usually had little consequence: only the previous year the setting up of a temporary Relief Committee to distribute bread for two weeks had proved sufficient to ensure that 'every excuse has now been taken away for disturbances such as have taken place in other large towns'.[22] But in January 1887 more than 500 of the unemployed were involved, and at the marketplace meeting both the League's speakers informed the crowd that the Lord Mayor had at least £300 in hand from the previous year's Distress Fund. These two were then delegated to call immediately upon the Mayor. But they were kept waiting and then had an unproductive meeting during which the Mayor, Sir Harry Bullard, referred to the unemployed as 'loafers'. Mowbray and Henderson returned to the marketplace to inform the crowd that 'the matter was then in their own hands'. This marked the beginning of the 'Battle of Ham Run'.[23] Food shops were looted and there were scuffles with the police, who arrested the two League speakers for incitement, additionally charging Mowbray with the offence of stealing a policeman's truncheon.[24] News of the arrests led to a protest meeting with an attendance estimated at 3,000 in the city the next day. This scale of the protest was impossible to maintain however, and within a week Henderson and Mowbray had been gaoled for four and nine months respectively. The two men received hard labour sentences. They were the last prisoners to spend time on the treadmill in Norwich gaol.

Subsequently the agitation among the unemployed faded. This may have been because yet another Relief Committee was established, alongside the Distress Committee, in which radicals such as Crotch and Burgess were prominent and which had the effect of dampening down protest by the unemployed themselves. In addition the Spring 'pick up' in the local clothing and building industries eased unemployment levels. And third, the League's own ability to channel protest further was diminished by the fact that two of its most prominent speakers were now in prison. Thus, while it was able to mobilise large numbers to celebrate Henderson's release on

16 May, with a demonstration followed by an evening meeting attended by over 150, the League could not sustain permanent organisation among the unemployed.[25]

At the time of this setback membership of the Norwich branch was still growing, exceeding 150, or more than 20% of the national membership, according to reports at the League's Third Annual Conference.[26] However, the emphasis of branch work now switched back to a second year's round of open-air meetings. More members simply meant the extension of Socialist League pitches to towns such as Wymondham, Cromer, Dereham and Diss, as well as in Norwich and its satellite villages. The new members supported these in a passive way, since the list of regular speakers hardly changed or grew beyond ten or a dozen stalwarts, and little other form of activity was offered.[27] In what might have been a significant development early in May 1887, much of the membership was involved in collecting money in support of the Northumberland miners' strike, a rare instance in which the League as an organisation focused upon the emerging Labour Movement.[28]

Fed upon a diet of meetings at which the momentum of the previous year was being lost, members began to lapse or take an interest in 'indoor agitation', arguing among themselves. Such argument can be productive, but nationally the League was already shedding those socialists willing to embrace electoral politics. And in Norwich the bulk of the branch, always opposed to parliamentarianism, moved towards anarchist positions. In May Norwich Socialist League invited Prince Kropotkin to address a public meeting in the city, following which the anarchist paper *Freedom* began to be sold alongside *The Commonweal*, and a group proclaiming 'No Organisation' emerged around Henderson.[29] Early in July Henderson himself spoke on 'Socialism and True Love' at a meeting which 'was received in ominous silence' according to a local reporter.[30] This led to a further rift within the branch.

Henderson was similarly prominent at the end of the month when the Liberal Party called a demonstration, to protest at coercion in Ireland on the occasion of a visit by Lord Salisbury to Norwich. Up to 5,000 'Gladstonians and working-men Liberals' attended a rally in the marketplace, but Henderson, calling for 'three groans for Salisbury' as the PMs entourage passed, attempted to lead an abortive march upon Conservatives meeting in St Andrew's Hall.[31] He and his supporters were ridden down by mounted police and arrested, though charges against him were subsequently dropped.

Whether or not this experience was a turning point for Henderson is debatable: he became much less active in the League, leaving it early in 1888 as he turned his attention to the question of Labour Representation.[32] Yet anarchist ideas remained predominant in the Norwich branch, with Mowbray, formerly Henderson's main opponent, now playing a leading role in what must by now have been a bizarre internal branch life.

In the spring and summer of 1888 the League continued its open-air meetings, the highlight being the delayed Morris and Besant rally on 18 August. But the size of this 'monster gathering' was testimony to the popularity of the two speakers generally, rather than to the specific influence of Norwich Socialist League, for its other meetings were much less well attended.[33] Similarly, while demonstrations of between 200 and 400 unemployed workers did occur from September 1887 to February 1888, there were no repeats of 'Ham Run', anarchist threats notwithstanding.[34] By the autumn of 1888 the League's one attraction was a public meeting to commemorate the trial and execution of the Chicago Anarchists, with Lucy Parsons, wife of one of those executed, speaking. This was followed by a series of lectures on 'the Philosophy of Anarchism' given by Mowbray.[35] From this point the Socialist League in Norwich ceased to be an organisation as such, though the now self-styled 'Anarchist-Communists' continued to meet in their Anarchist Hall rented, oddly enough, from councillor Hotblack, a prominent local Conservative politician and shoe manufacturer.[36]

As elsewhere, the effort to make socialists by the League in Norwich was brief and effectively at an end by the close of 1888. What was its impact upon the Labour Movement? Though the League had drawn many people to socialist ideas, its most glaring defect was its inability to suggest a second step on the road to socialism. For example, the possibility of organising in workplaces so that workers might use their collective strength, even if simply to defend League members faced with victimisation, seems not to have been considered. Because of its 'all or nothing' attitude, strikes and resistance to lock-outs were seen as worthy of support, but essentially as diversionary events. The League failed to built upon workers' own struggles, or even to see the potential in these.[37] Instead it offered the vision of a glorious future in the hope that those who accepted it, supposedly the very poorest and least organised, would then somehow stumble across the means of achieving it. Consequently, even though the League acted as a school for socialists, its ex-members, if they remained active, had no firm guidelines as to their subsequent conduct.

This is not to suggest that no lessons were learned by these individual socialists or that the League in Norwich was irrelevant. Political understanding and confidence are not quantifiable, but there can be little doubt that the League's ideas and vision gave many workers the stimulus to try their own hand at trade unionism or political activity. Henderson described, for example, how 'We carried on a continuous propaganda in the villages all around Norwich . . . in many of the villages we held a meeting once a week for a year, even two years. This work did much to prepare the way for a trade union in the countryside'.[38] It was more than coincidence that perhaps the strongest branch of the Navvies, Bricklayers, Labourers and General Labourers Union in Norfolk was formed in 1886 in St Faith's, the village where the Socialist League had a branch for two years. The League's propaganda campaigns may also have affected the Norwich radicals, whose successful efforts in electing the 'independent socialist' Crotch as an alternative to their sitting Liberal councillor occurred shortly after its first series of open air meetings in the autumn of 1886.[39] And more specifically, the influence of former League members on supporters in the Independent Labour Party and trade unions can be traced, as several were to become key figures in the labour movement. Thus C. Reynolds, a plasterer, was a founder member of Norwich Trades Council in 1886, while A. Sutton and G.F. Hipperson were both elected Secretary to that body, respectively in 1897 and 1906. Sutton and H. Witard were founder members of Norwich ILP in 1894, with Witard becoming the ILP's first councillor and perhaps the leading figure in Norwich Labour Party during the First World War.

With hindsight, Henderson was to suggest, 'The younger workers who were caught up in this movement were wise enough and far-sighted enough to see that, while such propaganda of idealist purposes was a vital source of energy and inspiration for action, what was needed was a much more definite organisation of working class power in the city'.[40] While there might be some truth in this analysis, the impression that the young ex-League activists moved as one is certainly erroneous, and Henderson's own behaviour in his last year of membership was hardly a model of clarity. After 1888 the attempt to make socialists continued, but was subordinated to the question of organisation, whether in the unions, in an 'advanced radical' section in the Liberal Party or, later, in the ILP. Before 1888 these alternatives were much less obvious and the League itself had no organised bodies around which it could work. Radical stirrings within the Liberal Party had reached an early peak in 1886, and indeed the League may have had some impact on these. Trade unionism was weak in terms of numbers and organisation. The one major industrial dispute occurring in Norwich during the years in which the League was a force came very late, in February 1888, in the shape of a lock-out at Haldenstein's shoe works involving 120 workers.[41] Agitation among the unemployed had been attempted, with little success. In these circumstances the League's tendency to look to meetings rather than forms of struggle can be understood, even though it was increasingly less justifiable as the signs of a 'new' trade unionism became apparent, and even though it proved to be a crucial weakness.

The League's legacy was thus passed on through the commitment to socialism generated among its former members, a poor reward relative to the original aims and activity. Its various forms can be traced via the 'public figures', those whose names were recorded as, for example, councillors or trade union officials, or those mentioned in the radical press. More numerous but inaccessible were the unknown supporters who figured among the rank and file of the unions, radicals, or ILP. In turning our attention to these, we can only speculate upon the impact that the Socialist League had upon their development, and upon what might have been achieved had the growing Norwich branch of 1885-7 existed in the more favourable circumstances of 1889-92, when the masses who had stood in the marketplace or around other League pitches were drawn into activity. Considering its aims, the League's inability to prolong even its own existence as a socialist organisation into a period of rising struggle was failure indeed.

3

Upsurge and Downturn

Trade Unionism in the late 1880s and 1890s

In Norwich as elsewhere the 'New Unionism' of the semi- and unskilled workers was to be a major feature in the upsurge in trade union activity around 1890. It was preceded by the establishment of new unions on a small scale, by the reorganisation of some local bodies, and by the formation of a Trades Council, in which skilled unions played a leading role. In October 1885, for example, leaflets and letters to the press announced a meeting of trade unionists to receive a report from a 'Norwich delegate' to the Trades Union Congress.[1] From this meeting a committee was elected 'to prepare a scheme for a United Trades Council' and, rather ambitiously, an invitation sent to the TUC suggesting that a future Congress might be held in Norwich.[2]

At a more modest level local trade unionism arose in a variety of ways. Sometimes it developed out of industrial disputes, for instance in November 1885 when weavers at Hovells Furnishings refused to work for less than customary rates. Deputations persuaded local employers to draw up an agreed series of rates and prices for work and this success led to the formation of the Horse Hair Weavers Union. Significantly the new union was assisted by the Shoemakers Society, the Handloom Weavers Society and the proto-Trades Council. Women members were recruited and also involved in the organisation of the union.[3] Similarly in the shoe industry demands for an agreed scale of rates for work and a recognised procedure for arbitration in 1885 helped revitalise the independent Norwich Fitters and Rivetters, which was re-formed as part of the National Union of Rivetters and Fitters in August 1886. The Norwich branch then took industrial action in January 1887, recruiting more members in the process, as well as at a series of related public meetings.[4] In addition, the Navvies, Bricklayers' Labourers and General Labourers Union had begun to enrol labourers and farmworkers after its secretary, John Ward, had completed a speaking tour in and around Norwich in 1885. In the next three years the union formed branches in Norwich and in St Faith's, where some of the membership had already held a strike by 1888.[8]

Decisive steps forward for trade unionism in terms of numerical growth were taken in 1889, and of strike activity in 1890. The year 1889 opened with further reorganisation of trade unions in the shoe industry, with the formation of the Norwich Clickers Mutual Benefit Society and Trade Union and closed with the entry of this body, some 200 strong, into the national Boot Clickers and Rough Stuff Cutters.[6] A more significant development, however, was the formation of a local general trade union in November, initially called the Norfolk and Norwich Labour Union. This was actually a 'residual' union recruiting in all occupations, including women workers and 'Skilled artisans who from health, age, distance of nearest branch of other sufficient reasons are unable to join the recognised unions belonging to their respective trades'.[7] As more than twenty skilled trade unions already had branches in Norwich by this time, the NNLU was not attractive to skilled workers, but it made a brisk beginning among the unskilled, including women. A separate women's branch was formed in May 1890, and this had 200 members by the end of June.[8] Village branches had been established among smiths, labourers and farmworkers in Sprowston, Thorpe, Plumstead and Poringland, with the result that Burgess, a vice-president of the union felt, '. . . that no trade union had ever made such rapid progress in this part of the country as the NNLU ... it is quite expected that on celebration of the [First] Anniversary it will number something like 1,000 members'.[10] When the NNLU merged with another local body, the Cromer based Norfolk Federal Union in January 1891, the combined membership of the new Norfolk and Norwich Amalgamated Labour Union was actually over 2,000.[11]

Such progress was not achieved without a price, and the rapidity of the NNALU expansion brought it into conflict with other, nationally organised, general unions. As well as the Navvies Union, the Gasworkers and General Labourers Union had appeared in Norwich in 1889, and the General Railway Workers Union in 1890. On questions of membership, attitude to strikes and political affinities the local and nationally based bodies clashed. In the summer of 1890 the Gasworkers Union, which already had a women's branch of its own, accused the NNLU of poaching from 'a bigger and better union'. Its men's branch, based upon the local gas works, had grown rapidly after December 1889, benefiting from the London settlement made by the British Gaslight Company, which also owned the Norwich works. But union members were picked off, or placed upon less regular work, which led to a decline in membership by May, and though thirty-seven members struck in July they were beaten.[12] The NNLU could not be blamed for these difficulties, but the Gasworkers Union was under pressure, and allegations concerning its funds by the locally-based rival did not help. Only after the spectacle of a public debate in Norwich marketplace between Will Thorne and Edmund Burgess, in which the alleged characteristics of local workers as well as forms of trade union organisation came to the fore, did the speakers belatedly agree 'to bury the hatchet . . . as there was better work to do in the interest of the Labour Movement'.[13]

Whether or not the NNALU 'poached' members, it did recruit from smaller unions exhausted by disputes. In September 1890, for example, the United Wire Netting Weavers Union, a local body with around 100 members, had gone on strike at Boulton and Paul, its members refusing to work with an ex-member. After a month the union was beaten and some members re-employed in batches '. . . personally selected by Mr Paul who doubtless feels some satisfaction that he has succeeded in greatly weakening, if not altogether destroying, the union'.[14] The survivors then were absorbed into the NNALU, forming a Wire Workers branch in January 1891. Similarly the NNALU had a less than robust attitude to strikes and to anything bordering on the controversial in political matters. As early as December 1890 it began to lose farmworker members, allegedly because it paid little attention to agricultural questions. When faced with direct provocation from Sprowston farmers in the form of a 1/- wage reduction, it took the novel step of paying its affected members the deducted shilling from union funds, rather than taking any form of industrial action.[15] And when calls for independent Labour representation began to be made at union branches in 1890, these, it was later revealed, were stifled. Burgess, then President of the NNALU, recalled that when the union '. . . threatened to become too independent of the Liberal Party . . . through the good offices of George Edwards one or two trusty Liberals were introduced to the union - to give it "tone" as it were'.[16] If the union was growing on the basis of enrolments rather than action and upon an ostensibly 'non-political' stance, its reasoning was that the recruitment of members took first priority, for

'... if these had not been enrolled they would have been outside the ranks of trade unionism today'.[17] More importantly it was stated that the union was founded '... upon a new principle altogether ... strikes had been a failure. They hoped to bring about a system by which they could settle disputes ... by arbitration or conciliation'.[18] Such hopes, reflecting the Liberal influences behind the NNALU, were to prove unfounded.

While trade unionism among skilled workers continued to expand slowly early in 1890, with branches of the Amalgamated Society of Housepainters and Decorators and of the Typographical Association being formed,[19] more rapid strides were made by another new union, the General Railway Workers. This was effectively the first union among railway workers in the Norwich area, partly because its subscription rates were lower than those of the Amalgamated Society of Railway Servants. Assisted by the Trades Council, it recruited on the basis of demands for a shorter working week. This was linked with other trade union and socialist demands for the Eight Hour Day and produced, for example, a mass meeting in the city centre at the end of May variously estimated at between 2,000 and 6,000. In itself this indicated the growth of interest in trade union aims, and the GRWU had now recruited 230 members.[20] The campaign for a shorter working day stopped short of strike action and failed to win concessions but, just as it was fading, by far the biggest dispute seen in Norwich to date began in the shoe industry.

The Rivetters and Finishers, part of the national union since 1886, had been improving their union organisation and taking sporadic strike action, and in June 1890 they demanded extra payment for extra work throughout the city. For their part the Norwich manufacturers had been expecting more complex work to be completed at old rates, and, watching the union's growth, had signed bonds of £100 each pledging themselves to stand together.[21] All this compounded the sense of grievance and as many as 6,000 shoeworkers came out on strike, with at least 1,000 more laid off. Further, 'the most remarkable feature ... is that non-union men are making common cause with the union hands and are turning out in quite as large a proportion as organised workers'.[22] Union members on 12/- per week strike pay were solid, while collections and donations financed weekly payments for non-union members.[23] With no prospect of an early or large-scale return to work the employers made concessions on women's and girls' shoes, the bulk of the controversial work, and the strike ended on 14 July. It was not a complete victory but a major step forward, and in the two weeks following the strike a further 300 or 400 workers joined the union.[24] Moreover, the wave of confidence among shoeworkers was sustained at a high level. When, immediately before Christmas, Haldensteins' reneged on the piece-work agreements and refused to accept conciliation procedures, the workers directly affected struck and were joined by hundreds more on 27 December. A bitter nine-week strike followed, involving 595 workers, until the employer agreed to recognise the local Arbitration Board and to return to previous piece-work rates.[25]

In Norwich 1891 proved to be a peak year for industrial disputes, but the willingness of trade unionists to take strike action was not the only factor. Resistance from local employers became more determined and there were also difficulties in sustaining union growth and integrating the new members. Moreover the divisions of sex, craft and job-demarcation remained, and these were compounded by the conciliatory attitude and loose organisation of the NNALU. In January S.D. Page and Son, brushmakers in Norwich and Wymondham, introduced new machinery for boring out brushheads and imposed new piece-work rates, which effectively cut wages by 12 to 15%. Members of the Amalgamated Society of Brushworkers in Norwich came out on strike and were summarily dismissed. They were joined by women workers in Wymondham who, upon finding that they received substantially less pay than women at the Norwich works, formed a second women's branch of the NNALU. Strike breakers were brought in and this led to clashes at the end of February. With the gaoling of two strikers for 'following in a disorderly manner' a blackleg, early in March, there was a protest demonstration in Norwich involving no fewer than 6,000 people.[26] Eventually the employers agreed to reinstate the sacked skilled men and to re-negotiate rates and operative procedures on the new machinery in Norwich. At this point members of the Brushmakers Society returned to work, leaving the forty-six women members of the NNALU in Wymondham to return on whatever basis they could obtain. At least twenty of the women were still locked out at the end of October, without financial assistance from their own union, as 'their subscriptions had been absorbed in the union's general expenses', an issue promptly seized upon by both the Gasworkers and Navvies Unions.[27]

Similar weaknesses were revealed in a major dispute in the local building industry. In February 1891 the skilled Operative Bricklayers

Society had submitted a pay claim for an additional 1d per hour, being joined in this by the two labourers' unions, the Navvies and the NNALU. Strike action began on 4 May, but some employers had already agreed to raise skilled rates from 6d to 7d per hour and on these sites the OBS men returned to work, leaving the labourers' claim unsolved. During May the leaders of the NNALU recommended their members to return to work for an extra halfpenny per hour where this could be obtained, alleging that they had been let down by the OBS. But their own action undermined the Navvies Union which was holding out for the full 1d. And NNALU members were also trying to return to work on sites where the OBS was still in dispute. Without work or strike pay they were in a weak position, poorly led and posing further problems for the Navvies Union.

This was the backcloth for renewed inter-union quarrelling and more street debates in June 1891.[28] While the NNALU leaders preached conciliation, Ward, for the Navvies, stressed that his union was not going to settle for 4d per hour in Norwich when members in the north-west of England were already earning 5d. Referring to the advantages of national organisation, central funds and strike pay, he added that in Norwich, 'They had a local union (NNALU) and of course it could not possibly overcome even the first crisis. The masters knew the limited resources at their disposal'.[29] Not until the Amalgamated Society of Carpenters and Joiners and the Stonemasons joined the dispute in mid-June did the employers agree to arbitration, and even then the result was inconclusive. The skilled unions accepted a halfpenny per hour rise with a shorter winter working week and the promise of a similar rise in another three months. However, the Navvies Union had to join the NNALU in accepting a settlement which raised labourers' rates from 3½d to 4d.[30] This dispute, involving more than 500 craftsmen and a larger number of labourers, had revealed trade union divisions and exposed the differing approaches of the labourers' unions. Significantly, by October the Navvies were growing and recruiting particularly among ex-members of the NNALU.[31]

Any attempt to assess the impact of trade unionism in Norwich between 1889-91 has to begin by recognising the extent of trade union growth. There were more than 900 skilled trade unionists, since the known membership in nine of the local branches was 858.[32] The secretary of the National Union of Boot and Shoe Operatives branch claimed '1,000 men' in 1895, which was likely to be lower than the figure for 1890-1 when the then Rivetters and

Finishers Union had successfully taken strike action.[33] The Norwich sections of the NNALU had approximately 1,200 members, nearly all unskilled, while there were 230 members in the GRWU.[34] As these combined figures suggest a total membership of 3,300, which does not include the unknown but sizeable memberships of the Gasworkers and Navvies Unions, it is likely that the true figure was in excess of 3,500, and possibly closer to 4,000. On the lower figure, and assuming that three out of every four 'Norwich' trade unionists worked in or very close to Norwich, a 10% trade union density among male workers can be derived from 1891 census data.[35] Given the adverse aspects of the industrial and occupational structure previously outlined, this was impressive enough. Moreover, there were a number of disputes in which a considerable level of activity and participation can be detected, while national issues such as the Eight Hour Day were enthusiastically taken up. This was the theme of the first real May Day demonstration held in Norwich in 1891, which coincided with the brushmakers' strike and the beginning of the strike in the building industry. Estimated at between 2,200 and 5,000, and watched by a crowd of up to 10,000 strong, this was 'The largest and most important trade union demonstration of any kind ever held in Norwich'.[36]

May Day 1891 was the first high water-mark for trade unionism. Shortly afterwards the brushworkers and building disputes ended in partial, flawed victories and there were no more strikes that year. Instead, the employers took the initiative in a reportedly depressed labour market.[37] In August, Howes, a leading building firm, reduced labourers' wage rates and announced that they would not employ trade union members. The same month the City Corporation cut wages for labourers on its sewerage construction scheme, and Haldensteins began to erode the agreements made after the strike earlier in the year.[38] With its diversity of membership and uncertainty of approach, the NNALU was particularly vulnerable. In a neat example of class struggle between adherents to the Liberal Party, NNALU members were victimised at Colmans, while the inability of the union to resist wage cutting by local farmers meant the loss of agricultural branches, first in Plumstead then in Poringland. Its women's branch in Wymondham had now collapsed, while some of its most active women members in Norwich were victimised at Harmer's clothing factory after trying to resist a 20% wage cut.[39] In six disastrous months the total NNALU membership fell by two-thirds from 2,500 to just 840.[40]

Though other unions were not as badly affected, a loss of momentum in numbers and activity was discernible at the beginning of 1892. In the shoe industry 'several hundred members have run out of membership' it was claimed, all but wiping out NUBSO's gains of 1890. Simultaneously the separatist Clickers' 'Mutual Benefit Society' continued its drift into obscurity.[41] The Navvies Union called a series of public meetings to raise interest in a 6d per hour wage claim to equal the London rate, but reckoned in terms of two years' preparation for strike action.[42] Not surprisingly the belated May Day demonstration was a comparatively timid affair: 'Most of the unions have fallen off in numbers very considerably since last year . . . the NNALU and the railway workers' union have both decreased . . . and of those members who remain true . . . the proportion who turned up to take part in the demonstration was very small in comparison to last year's turnout'.[43] There were no strikes of any size in 1892 and only one, a brief dispute over piece-work rates at Hales' shoeworks, in 1893.[44] In similar vein early in 1894 the management at Boulton and Paul took advantage of the decline of trade union activity there to cut wages by up to one third in the wire drawing department when introducing new machinery. Employee resistance was broken by an effective lockout.[45]

By the time TUC delegates assembled in Norwich for the 1894 Conference local union organisation was therefore much weakened. Only the printing industry, where a branch of the Bookbinders and Machine Rulers was established and where the Typographical Association continued to recruit, could be regarded as a growth area.[46] On the railways the decline of the GRWU was not offset by the founding of a branch of the Amalgamated Society of Engine Drivers and Firemen. Nor did the more general Amalgamated Society of Railway Servants make headway.[47] Similarly the efforts of the Navvies Union to recruit in the building industry were offset by the continuing decline of the NNALU while the strengthening of the Gasworkers and General Labourers sections at Colmans was paralleled by the loss of members in less concentrated pockets. Though not an entirely accurate guide to total trade union membership in the city, the number of trade unionists affiliated to the Norwich Trades Council had dropped from 3,000 in 1891 to 2,400 in 1893. While this revived to 2,699 in 1894, it no doubt reflected special efforts for, and interest in, TUC year; and the 1895 figure contracted to 2,155.[48]

The Trades Council, making preparations to host the TUC, was simultaneously feeling the need to hold public meetings in local schools 'to specially propagate the principles and advantages of trade and labour societies'. These meetings reflected the swing to an ultra cautious approach by the Council and the renewed domination of orthodox Liberal politics. Thus the Trades Council Chairman, Frank Delves, informed his audience that '. . . they had decided to keep politics entirely in the background . . . strikes they made a dead set against, and would only resort to in extreme cases. The Trades Council had initiated a scheme for arbitration and conciliation'.[49] Such attitudes typified the local aspects of the 1894 TUC, with Delves apologising for the relatively poor state of Norwich trade unionism in his address as President of the Congress. He cited the fact that Norwich was 'almost out of the industrial world' and pointed to the 'problems' of ex-agricultural labour and working women, in an account which entirely ignored the recent experiences of trade unions in the city and offered no practical solutions. Referring to farmworkers, he described how mechanisation and low wages '. . . sends them into our towns to flood our markets, keep down wages and hinder the work of organisation'.[50] In a speech to the TUC Women's Meeting he pointed out that equal pay was an essential aim, though he then said nothing about its realisation. Skating over the trade union contribution, he instead castigated the local Women's Liberal Association for 'having done practically nothing to elevate and organise the working women of Norwich'.[51]

Advice offered by the TUC itself was hardly better. At a special meeting on the subject of 'Trade Union Organisation', John Burns informed local trade unionists that if Norwich could support '500 pubs and a fat bookmaker at every corner' it could support trade unionism.[52] The Trades Council tried to draw maximum comfort from the formalities and junkets which accompanied the proceedings: 'We feel that the cordial reception extended to our friends by the capitalistic class is an indication that the time is fast passing away for the organised workers to be looked down on or regarded by the employers as their natural enemies . . . our policy is that which we claim viz Defence not Defiance'.[53] Conclusions like these did little to prepare local trade unionists for the struggles of the next few years.

Up to the turn of the century the trade union picture in Norwich had its similarities with the national one, most unions being on the defensive and making only occasional limited responses. Examples of this activity include a strike by twenty-five wire workers at Boulton and Paul against the introduction of fines for alleged waste in November 1896, a strike by young workers in the tinplate shops at Colmans over deteriorating conditions of work in August 1899, and a demarcation dispute between brickmakers and tilers on local building sites in 1898.[54]

Evidence of a counter-attack by employers similar to that of the early 1890s is not sustained. Rather, their range of approaches to trade unionism suggests they were firmly back in control. Wage cutting and changed methods of working, with or without the introduction of new machinery, were included in these. Some firms, for example Caleys the sweet manufacturer, were positively non-union, while others, such as Boulton and Paul, regularly attempted to snuff out trade union organisation. Wage bargaining at others, such as Colmans, was relatively sophisticated: having broken the NNALU presence in 1890, Colmans conceded no pay increases generally until 1899, instead attempting to limit a recruitment drive by the Gasworkers and General Labourers Union by offering selective pay rises to 'favoured' workers. Only when the union presence was sufficient to produce a solid, section-wide strike call, did Colmans make a further concession. This was a pay rise granted without any form of consultation with the union and paid only in sections where the union was known to be strong.[55]

An additional factor in local industrial relations was the employers' reluctance to participate in national bodies. Some simply wished to retain a free hand; others were not under such pressure from union militancy that they felt a need to combine in, say, the Federation of Boot and Shoe Manufacturers or the Engineering Employers Federation. Thus Norwich did not figure in the national shoe industry dispute of 1895 or in the lockout of engineering workers after the Amalgamated Society of Engineers' pay claim in 1897.[56] Yet the building and shoe industries were the scene of major confrontations in the late 1890s in Norwich. Each closely paralleled national developments and resulted in severe setbacks for local trade unionism.

The 'Home Boom' of the middle and late 1890s provided a favourable environment for trade union activity in the building industry nationally. In 1894 the trade in Norwich was picking up, and an extra 200 labourers were employed on a new sewerage construction and street repairs scheme by the City Corporation. In this situation the Navvies' union attempted to close the gap between London and Norwich wages, an issue around which it had been agitating for two years. Calling for a fifty-five-hour summer working week at a rate of 5d per hour, union speakers addressed a meeting of 800 labourers at the end of May. This was taken as the sounding board for a strike which began on 9 June. Over 500 labourers struck, but with inconclusive results. While some employers settled quickly on the new terms, more than 200 labourers were locked out. Those not in the union but supporting the strike were unable to last long on the basis of public donations and many returned to work by the end of June on the old conditions. This effectively ended city-wide strikes among building labourers for the rest of the 1890s.[57]

Thereafter, disputes were smaller and craft orientated. In May 1895 members of the Amalgamated Society of Housepainters and Decorators led a brief and partly successful strike, involving many non-union men, to obtain a rate of 5½d per hour.[58] But bricklayers attempting to raise their wages at a Norwich brewery in February 1896 were dismissed and replaced by non-union men.[59] Again in 1899 a strike by 200 labourers constructing the city's tramways failed to secure its objectives.[60] A strike by 176 ASHD members in 1901 ended in defeat after four months, despite conciliatory efforts by the Trades Council, and this proved a sharp setback for the union. And worse still, a strike by 300 bricklayers on forty sites, which began confidently enough on 1 June 1900 was not concluded for thirteen months. A minority of employers agreed to the union demands but, though the Operative Bricklayers Society levied members working at the new rates and found alternative work for many still on strike, it had lost the initiative. The dispute ended with a degree of victimisation, some employers paying only part of the original claim and others making no concessions.[62] Thus in the building industry a series of confrontations had led to some pay rises for craftsmen, but ultimately a series of reverses for their unions, while the labourers had been pushed on to the defensive.

In the shoe industry the setback was more sudden and dramatic, hinging upon the long strike of 1897. As in other shoemaking centres, the extension of mechanised production and attendant changes in labour methods in Norwich had led to a series of small disputes in the mid-1890s in which the National Union of Boot and Shoe Operatives enjoyed some degree of success. These included strikes in 1895 by 170 sew-round workers against the 'team' system, in which one or two workers on piece-work set the pace for others on fixed pay. There were also three strikes in 1896 over the introduction of new work patterns and piece-work rates without consultation.[63]

Norwich did not figure in the national lockout over pay and work processes in 1895, but local shoeworkers were keenly aware of its significance. At a series of meetings in October 1895 organised by NUBSO, the local branch President, W.R. Smith, discussed these, emphasising that 'the minimum wage away in other centres was the maximum in Norwich'. W. Votier, now a national figure in NUBSO and prominent in the Leicester Independent Labour Party, also spoke at these meetings. He pointed out that hostility to mechanisation itself was misdirected and that, 'If the men of Norwich were prepared to take the paltry wages they were receiving today, they would remain the blackspot on the country, a bugbear to the trade and a disgrace to themselves'.[64] Agitation for a minimum wage continued throughout 1896 despite an outright rejection by the manufacturers in January, and culminated in a mass meeting on 18 February 1897 which was intended as a springboard to strike action. At the outset it was stressed that the union claim was for the principle of a minimum wage and that the actual level, 28/- for clickers and 26/- for pressers and rough stuff cutters, could be submitted to arbitration.[65] Yet even at this meeting the dangers of entering a strike without the full participation of the other NUBSO branch of the rivetters and finishers were stressed. Moreover there were allegations that members had not fully been consulted and that there was 'wire pulling' to bring out Norwich workers in sympathy with those in Leicester, where a similar dispute was in progress. Whether true or not, these accusations were indicative of a less than solid beginning to the strike. Nearly 1,400 workers came out initially and, with the failure of arbitration efforts at the end of February, numbers and the level of militancy began to rise. Around 1,500 strikers, accompanied by 'a huge crowd' of spectators, demonstrated outside each of the main shoe works early in March.[66]

Though some smaller employers offered to concede, the main ones were determined to sit out the dispute. Non-union members increasingly gave up the strike and, as work was also being subcontracted to garret masters, some levels of output were maintained even when rivetters and finishers joined the stoppage on 10 April. At a stormy public meeting on 18 May both the NUBSO branch secretaries, Mason and Folkhard, expressed their regret that the strike had ever begun. Later, at a solidarity demonstration called by the Trades Council on 12 June, Tom Mann, as principal speaker, made the now unhelpful point that the strike would have gone better had the union recruited more members before it began.[67] In August the employers rebuffed a third Mayoral intervention and only on 19 October was a provisional agreement reached after negotiations at the Board of Trade. This involved pay rises of up to 5% for some workers, but the employers made no concessions on the question of a minimum wage. Worse, it was agreed that 'it shall not be a condition of resuming work that all men shall be reinstated'.[68]

Such terms, signed over the heads of the strikers by Inskip, the union General Secretary, in London on 22 October, produced consternation in Norwich. Three hundred strikers marched to the home of J. Mason, the local union Secretary, to demand no settlement on these terms, while at the mass meeting called on 23 October there was, according to one local paper, 'a spirit of violent dissatisfaction at what one of the speakers described as "the disastrous termination of the struggle"'.[69] The defeat suffered by the union was conclusive. Over 200 members were not reinstated and both Smith and Mason were victimised.[70] NUBSO membership in Norwich fell from 800, at the start of the strike, to roughly 400 over the next two years.[71] For the shoeworkers, these were deep wounds: there was no major dispute in the Norwich shoe industry for more than a decade.

The impact of such bitter defeats on trade unionism generally in Norwich is easy enough to imagine but difficult to quantify. Yet if, by 1900, trade unionism appeared more marginal in Norwich and much less strong than in some other parts of Britain, this was not an inevitable outcome. What had been some key parts of a previously emerging and growing trade union movement had been subjected to a series of severe blows. Thus interpretations of trade union weakness arising from apathy on the part of Norwich workers cannot adequately explain the course of events over the 1890s. Moreover, in other ways the local Labour Movement continued to develop. Support for a separate and specific Labour Party, or for a distinct labour presence within the Liberal Party, already existed in the 1880s. Around 1890, however, these ideas began to be aired regularly before trade union audiences, meeting with growing interest. At the subdued May Day celebrations of 1892 there were trade union, Liberal and Socialist platforms and, 'From the beginning to the end of the speechmaking, the Socialist meeting maintained the premier position in point of numbers'.[72] Similarly if the TUC had done relatively little to stimulate trade unionism in Norwich, the presence of up to eighty delegates who were members or supporters of the new ILP did have an effect, as will be seen.

Would workers' overt political activity prove a complement or an alternative to trade unionism and industrial struggle? In Norwich , against a background of industrial defeats and trade union weaknesses, workers were likely to switch their attention to the apparently more rewarding process of electioneering. While the brand of labour representative still had to be determined, other fundamental questions were not fully discussed. Direct activity in the workplace tended to be neglected by those who sought to win votes through resolutions or to deliver trade union votes *en masse* for the party of their choice. In such ways trade union weakness was compounded and the socialism which emphasised workers' collective struggles at the workplace was further eclipsed. Could electoral politics atone for these shortcomings in organisation and orientation, which had now become a feature of the Norwich Labour Movement?

4

Liberal or Labour?
Labour Representation up to 1903

The second half of the 1880s saw not only the efforts of socialists to make converts and build organisations, but also a revival of interest in forms of Labour Representation. Whether the latter became more attractive on a national scale precisely because of the failure of the Social Democratic Federation and the Socialist League to expand rapidly, or because its own objectives seemed more attainable in the short term, there was a considerable overlap of trade union and labour representation activity. Nationally this was formalised in the establishment of a Labour Electoral Committee by the TUC in 1886.[1] Though the body which developed from this, the Labour Electoral Association, in practice went little further than the Labour Representation League of the 1870s in building a movement genuinely independent of the Liberal Party, the possibility of independent Labour candidates was posed.[2] The issue sharpened after 1888, when Keir Hardie contested the Mid-Lanark by-election as 'Labour and Home Rule' candidate. And as it aroused working class support, the efforts of the Liberal Party in particular to maintain its own influence in the stirring Labour Movement became more urgent.

While radicals and trade unionists had been elected as Liberal local councillors in Norwich as early as 1886, their demands for a parliamentary candidate first surfaced in 1888. On 26 May 1888 a meeting was held in protest at the conduct of Liberal councillors and their misrepresentation of the radical viewpoint. Although the isolationist stance adopted by the Norwich Socialist League meant that socialists did not play a central role in the meeting, loyalty to the Liberal Party was questioned.[3] The possibility of a rival organisation was not discussed, but threats to withdraw voting support were made. An editorial in *Daylight* warned, 'It is as well there should be no misunderstanding as to the attitude of working Liberals of Norwich who, if they cannot alone win an election, can by their abstention certainly mar one'.[4] This was a dangerous state of affairs for both the Liberal 'Grandees' and the more loyal working-class Liberals. They attempted to lower the political temperature by producing a scheme for 'a genuine Labour candidate' to accompany the existing Liberal MP, J.J. Colman. But while local Liberal leaders had made this concession by December 1888 they were unwilling to take further action until forced to do so. With no prospect of an immediate General Election and with the trade union upsurge commanding the attention of many working-men Liberals, matters did not come to a head until 1891. By then several branches of the Norwich and Norfolk Amalgamated Labour Union had passed resolutions requesting that a 'Direct Labour' candidate should stand as a second Liberal. It was even rumoured that Ben Tillett would be selected.

There was some substance in this speculation, though it was also public knowledge that 'A considerable section of the Liberal Party are the reverse of anxious for a direct Labour candidate'.[5] Liberals on the local Trades Council were told that Tillett had been approached, but was unwell and could not therefore be considered. This explanation avoided the real issue, highlighted by Tillett himself in a letter to Burgess. 'I . . . should be prepared to undertake any work which would mean the material advancement of social questions. I should be prepared to represent Norwich providing I was allowed to state my principles without subordinating them to party officialism'.[6] In August and September there were further meetings of 'advanced radicals', with renewed talk of independent positions and indeed of a separate 'Labour Party'.[7] In this, Fred Henderson, the ex-Socialist League member, played a prominent role via the Norfolk and Norwich Labour Electoral Association. This organisation 'specifically requested that only bona fide working men attend' its meetings.[8] At one of these, Henderson declared, 'If there were only a dozen strong men in Norwich . . . who saw their way before them and said "We are going to form the nucleus of an independent position" they would cause such a difference in the relation of political parties . . . as had not been seen for a considerable time'.[9] Yet it was characteristic of Henderson that he did not break with Liberalism or permeationist ideas. His was not the call for an independent Labour Party. And in the event, neither the Labour Electoral Association members nor other radicals had any knowledge of, let alone choice in, the selection of James Bedford as an appropriate 'Labour' candidate by the senior Liberal Party figures.

In September 1891 Bedford was presented to the Norwich electorate as a working tailor from East London who was both President of the General Railway Workers Union and a trade unionist approved by the Labour Electoral Association and the Norwich Trades Council. Unfortunately for the holder of such impeccable credentials, a former member of Norwich Socialist League, Charles Mowbray, was himself a member of the Amalgamated Society of Tailors living in the East End. He wrote to *The Commonweal* pointing out that Bedford was the owner of a tailoring business and a 'sweater' into the bargain. Ignoring Bedford's threats of litigation, Mowbray returned to Norwich and challenged Bedford to a public debate, from which the latter's absence spoke volumes.[10] In an effort to offset such allegations, Bedford publicly replied to inquiries from the Trades Council, asserting that he had been a trade unionist 'for very many years, in principle', though his only trade union link was his two years' Honorary Presidency of the GRWU.[11]

By the end of October *Daylight* had received a resolution from the United Radical Club in East London 'calling upon workmen to repudiate Bedford's candidature in the interests of labour'. It also reported that socialists and 'not a small number of Liberals' were shouting down Bedford at Liberal ward meetings.[12] Feeling on the issue ran high in November, when the local Secretary of the Amalgamated Society of Tailors addressed a two-thousand-strong meeting in the city. Bedford was invited and again he failed to attend. Not surprisingly, the assembly resolved '. . . that Bedford is not a fit and proper person to represent us in the House of Commons, and that he be requested to withdraw and make room for a genuine Labour candidate'.[13] Finally, in the months preceding the General Election of July 1892, details of the Tillett affair became common knowledge, the Labour Electoral Association struck Bedford from its list of suitable candidates, and there were physical clashes between pro- and anti-Bedford Liberals.[14]

Whether such events had a direct bearing on the overall election result in Norwich is doubtful. The solitary Conservative candidate headed the poll and many of the workers concerned with the Bedford issue were still unenfranchised. Nevertheless, there was an appreciable difference of 600 votes between the two Liberal candidates.[15] Within a week of the election result a meeting of Trades Council delegates and radicals in the new Workingmen's Radical Club was affirming the need to prepare for a genuine direct Labour candidate. That autumn a third 'Lib/Lab' councillor,

J. Williment, was elected in the working-class Heigham ward.[16] Encouraging the radicals further, the Secretary of the London Democratic Club wrote to the Norwich press to congratulate '... the small body of staunch men whose honest growl has managed to upset Jimmy Bedford. Now must Norwich follow the glorious example of Middlesboro', Battersea and West Ham and select and elect their own man'.[17] Yet many of the 'advanced radicals' in Norwich remained unclear as to the precise method of doing this, having so far demonstrated only their unwillingness to have a phoney candidate foisted upon them. They were soon given the opportunity to make a more positive choice.

As in many other areas outside the north of England there was no swift reaction in Norwich to the formation of the Independent Labour Party in 1893. It was predicted that 'The ILP will do more for the working masses during the next five years than the Tory and Liberal parties combined have done for them within the last half century'.[18] But local figures such as Henderson, Mason and Williment, who were respectively identified by Liberals and much of the Labour Movement with socialist ideas, trade unionism and advanced radicalism, made no moves in the direction of the ILP. Instead the Norwich ILP branch was formed after public meetings coinciding with the 1894 TUC conference in the city. There, Tom Mann had claimed there were eighty delegates who supported the new Party.[19] Initially there were eighty-nine members, 'amongst them ... some of the advanced Radical Party in Norwich'. These were mainly ex-Socialist League members, who had left as the League veered off in an anarchist direction, or trade union activists. Prominent among the latter were J. Gardiner, Secretary of the Amalgamated Society of Tailors, Bill Holmes of the NNALU, F.J. Hoult from the United Society of Boilermakers and A. Jordan of the Typographical Association.[20]

However Norwich ILP was not at first able to build upon this promising foundation. Because the branch's orientation from the start was towards elections, the process of vote gathering quickly proved a stern test for a new and still small organisation to undertake. Moreover, this was always likely to induce a dilution of the socialism in the ILP appeal to voters if early results were not encouraging. Within a matter of weeks the ILP stood F.J. Hoult as a candidate in the Heigham ward municipal elections, and made a reasonable show in polling 262 votes against a Liberal Unionist who had Conservative support. Three other ILP members fared less well, however, when faced with Liberal and radical opponents in Poor Law Guardian elections.[21]

Compounding these early problems, the ILP soon had a competitor notionally to its left, which made any playing down of socialist ideas risky if the loyalties of existing socialist members were not to be strained. Though the Social Democratic Federation had never gone the distance with the Socialist League in Norwich in the 1880s, its new branch, formed in 1894, had a similar social composition to the ILP and proved as durable.[22] Its first intervention came in the 1894 local elections, when meetings called to discuss the ILP municipal programme also had to deal with extra demands raised by SDF members.[23]

However, it was in the General Election of 1895 that the SDF made its mark in the city and put the ILP under considerable pressure. The Liberals, on the defensive nationally against a growth in Tory support, had locally presented the ILP with two hostages to fortune. Eager to avoid repetition of the Bedford affair, they ran no 'working-man' candidate. F.W. Verney was described as 'out of touch with local radicals' and the other Liberal candidate, T.C. Terrell, was a London lawyer.[24] Moreover, Frank Delves, one of their leading trade unionists and President of the Trades Council was censured by that body after he invited the Liberal candidates to address it without proper authorisation.[25] Meanwhile the ILP was trying to take a contending position. In May, Tom Mann had spoken on 'The ILP as a Political Force' at a meeting designed to build support for a Norwich election campaign, and advertisements were placed for an election fund.[26] But with the failure of these efforts the ILP lost the initiative to the SDF, which now held its own public meetings, regularly intervened in both Liberal and Conservative meetings, and issued a series of leaflets urging workers to abstain from voting.[27] The SDF, according to the Liberal trade union paper, was thus 'showing signs of exceptional activity of late'.[28] In contrast, the ILP branch fragmented. Some of its more active members were working with the SDF, but when the ILP issued its own 'abstain' leaflet in the middle of July, its municipal election candidate and a number of others resigned, Hoult returning to Liberal platforms as a 'trade union' speaker.[29]

With the Conservative election victory the ILP came under new, sometimes hysterical, attacks from disappointed Liberals, while the SDF, itself no model of socialist purity, continued to pose problems[30] Though it had not been a critical factor in the Norwich election results, the call for abstention at the polls by the ILP hardly attracted Liberal-voting radicals, and was used by Liberal figures in the trade unions in attempts to discredit the new Party. Thus George Edwards, the NNALU Secretary, and seen by many as a 'moderate' working man, wrote, 'I look upon the leaders of the ILP as the greatest enemies that the Labour movement has today in England, and they have done more in the last few weeks to fasten the millstone around the neck of Labour than all the landlords and capitalists have done for the last ten centuries'.[31]

In reality the ILP was, as yet, no threat to the Liberals or Conservatives. But, bereft of any MPs after the 1895 General Election, the ILP had lost a key advantage it had claimed over the SDF. The latter appeared the tougher and more coherent of the two socialist bodies. In an effort to boost the local ILP branch, G.N. Barnes, who had been the ILP parliamentary candidate for Rochdale, came to Norwich at the end of August on a speaking tour. But in fact, his particular version of moralism and pragmatism was so much grist to the SDF mill. Interviewed by the *Eastern Weekly Leader* Barnes said, 'Hyndman sometimes says of splendid old Hardie that he knows nothing of economics. Well what of that? Hang economics! Let us get our constituency first, then we will begin to apply ourselves to the details of Acts of Parliament'.[32] Rather than bolstering the ILP, this produced a series of counter-meetings from the SDF. That autumn there were no ILP candidates in the municipal or Guardians' elections, the party instead concentrating upon basic educational meetings for its members.[33] Norwich ILP probably reached its lowest point at this time. With no national election successes, and losing members locally to the Liberals and the SDF, the possibility of fusion with the SDF as part of a Socialist Unity campaign was discussed. Indeed, the branch secretary later admitted there had been meetings '. . . to decide whether they should carry on the branch or not, as the outlook was not hopeful, being heavily in debt and the membership having fallen off'.[34]

For much of 1896 and 1897 Norwich ILP seemed to be sustained by the appearances of national figures. Hardie, MacDonald and Curran each addressed modest meetings, the audiences 'usually composed of the most thoughtful sections of workers, with a fair sprinkling of enquiring ladies'.[35] Membership was recovering, and a meeting addressed by Tom Mann in Norwich marketplace in August 1896 was said to be the largest socialist gathering since the Besant/Morris visit in 1888.[36] But the SDF competed strongly for wider support, bringing speakers such as Lansbury and

Hyndman to Norwich. Its meetings were similarly 'composed for the most part of working men'.[37]

Determining the respective strengths of the two organisations at this time is no clear-cut issue, especially when both seem to have missed opportunities. In the autumn of 1896 the ILP confined its electoral efforts to School Board Elections, with its candidate obtaining a respectable, albeit inadequate, vote based on the non-sectarian ticket.[38] This in itself was no failure, but the absence of either ILP or SDF candidates in municipal elections the following year does suggest organisational and political weaknesses. For in 1897 the Tory and Liberal parties agreed not to oppose each other in local elections, jointly issuing posters which informed the electorate that 'they would avoid Municipal contests this year in the interests of harmony and of good government of the city'.[39] This arrangement was immediately opposed by those 'advanced radicals' who saw it simply as a device to exclude the selection of more working-men Liberal candidates. Yet the ILP and SDF did not fully exploit the situation by standing candidates against the unopposed Liberals or Tories. When presented with audiences at protest meetings organised by radicals early in October, the socialist interventions were weak. Thus in Heigham ward, where H.A. Day, a Fabian Society 'Progressive Workingman's Candidate' was standing, a solitary SDF member simply invited the 200 or so Liberals present to join his organisation.[40] And though the ILP declared its intention of standing a parliamentary candidate in Norwich at the next opportunity, and approached Tom Mann on this matter in July 1897, it was soon rumoured that Mann was not impressed by the Labour Movement in the city generally, nor with the local ILP specifically.[41]

If the eight months' shoeworkers' strike had been a factor in the lack of electoral contests in 1897, neither of the socialist bodies had made major gains from this. H. Sutton, an ILP member, was elected as Trades Council Secretary in place of a Liberal, G.H. Cleverley, during the dispute, but he failed to hold this position in 1898.[42]. The ILP suffered further defections, both to the SDF and the 'radical' Liberals, so that despite some recruitment, its membership remained about sixty strong.[43] However this now comprised a reliable core and those who were prominent in the branch, G.H. Roberts, W. Holmes and H.E. Witard, achieved a wider success.[44]

Having rented premises for use as a club the ILP again contested School Board elections in 1899, although this time on a basis which sharply differentiated it from the Liberals but won SDF support. Since the Education Act of 1870 the Liberals had campaigned against the use of government finances by the Church of England in its voluntary schools and for the option of non-denominational religious instruction in State schools. But G.H. Roberts turned attention away from religious affairs. Announcing 'we shall neither ask nor expect favour from either of the orthodox parties', he stood on a programme which called for the raising of the school leaving age to sixteen years, free maintenance for all school children, and an upper classroom size of thirty.[45] These reforms, which were to be financed from graduated taxation, rather than the local rates, were seen as unrealistic by most of the Liberals. The SDF viewed them 'as definitely and outspokenly socialist as any of us could wish'. In the event Roberts was easily elected, coming sixth in the poll with over 11,000 votes. This was, as *Daylight* put it, 'An accomplishment with which the local socialists may well be proud ... the members of the ILP and SDF have worked like Trojans, and they have their reward'.[47] Such success inevitably raised confidence about the prospects for the ILP in Parliamentary elections.

Any dreams of popularity were rudely interrupted by the onset of the South African Wars, however. There was enough of a Liberal tradition in Norwich to avoid the worst excesses of jingoism but most Liberals initially attempted to dodge the issue or prepared to settle for a quick British victory. Only a small minority were willing to take an open anti-war stance. Early in 1900 a Norwich Peace Association was formed, mainly along religious and pacifist lines, but it was the SDF which took the lead locally in the Labour Movement by establishing a Workmen's Anti-War Committee at the end of April.[48] Both the SDF and ILP raised the issue at the 'Labour Carnival' on May Day, attracting sufficient support to enable the Workmen's Anti-War Committee to be reconstituted on a delegate basis, involving the Trades Council and radical Liberals. Interest was considerable. In a working-class radical ward such as Heigham, meetings were so large they could not be accommodated inside the Radical Club there. Significantly, a resolution passed at one open-air meeting here bore the imprint of the SDF, denouncing '... this capitalist war ... prosecuted for the financial gain of the same class against which English working men have to fight in matters of social reform and industrial questions at home'.[49] Ten months later the issue had become a major theme at the May Day Carnival, with W.R. Smith of the SDF and G.H. Roberts of the ILP making keynote speeches.[50]

More generalised opposition, based upon disillusionment with the war and its excesses, costs, or the delays in providing charitable funds for the dependants of soldiers, developed more slowly. Until this broadened into anti-Tory feeling, the socialists and campaigning radicals remained in a difficult situation. No doubt awareness of common ground on the anti-war question did encourage them to work together, but this was no one-way process. The SDF was particularly keen to contrast its efforts with the silence of prominent local Liberals, a factor intended to create tensions within radical ranks, and it is unlikely that all SDF or ILP members were totally immune from jingoistic pressures. Certainly it was known that the ILP had lost members, while the remaining ones much preferred to work around other issues.[51]

Around 1900 the ILP in Norwich was recovering, but its influence even upon local socialists was keenly contested by the SDF. The latter was performing equally well in efforts to weaken the Liberals' hold within the Norwich Labour Movement. After 1900 the formation of the Labour Representation Committee caused the realignment of some workers' loyalties, as did the growth of interest in the question of municipal control as a means of social improvement.[52] All the three parties, and indeed the Conservatives also, responded to these developments. But significantly each saw its struggle for influence primarily in electoral terms. There were conflicts over the nature and pace of social reform, but electoral contests virtually encapsulated the political activity locally. For the socialist organisations this had built-in disadvantages. Many workers, particularly the unskilled, those in rented accommodation, and women were unable to vote. Trade unionism and workplace activity, areas in which Liberal influence was more vulnerable, tended to be neglected or seen as ancillary to the mobilising of votes. Nevertheless, Labour, led by the ILP, grew in electoral strength in the early 1900s. Moreover, it did so at a time when the union movement in Norwich was relatively weak. How it was able to do this must therefore be explained.

5

Trade Unionism and Industrial Weakness, 1900-14

The opening years of the twentieth century marked a difficult period for trade unionism, nationally and locally. Unions were having to adjust to changes in work processes which undermined the bargaining position of many skilled workers, the bulk of trade union membership. Among unskilled workers, union organisation had been difficult to sustain over the 1890s in the face of unemployment, counter-measures by employers, and a string of hostile judicial decisions. All unions were on the defensive after the Taff Vale judgment of 1901, which made their funds a target for legal actions by employers, while there was both a steady deterioration in real wages and an increase in unemployment between 1900 and 1905.[1] In Norwich trade unionism had passed an early peak well before the defeats in the shoe industry dispute of 1897 and in the building industry in 1900-1.

There are few signs of local trade union recovery in the early 1900s. Only the strike in the printing industry in 1902 and the shoe industry dispute of 1908 involved workers in large numbers or on a city-wide basis. A handful of smaller conflicts were recorded in the local press, which, as it reported on these and national strikes in detail, can be taken as a reasonable guide to the extent of such activity. If the same could not always be said of Board of Trade coverage in these years, its *Labour Gazette* nevertheless had practically no items concerning disputes in Norwich, even though the Trades Council Secretary, Cleverley, was among those who regularly provided notes on employment levels and the state of particular trades.[2]

Further, the number of trade unionists affiliated to the Norwich Trades Council fell sharply, from 2,667 in 1899 to 1,576 in 1901 and to 1,200 in 1903, the pre-1900 affiliation figure not being regained until after 1910.[3] The significance of such a decline might be overstated if trade union branches simply affiliated a lower portion of their membership than in the past, or if they felt the Trade Council to be less representative of their views. But while the larger of the trade union branches covering the footwear industry remained unaffiliated until 1905, the total number of branches represented at the Trades Council tended to rise over the decade, from nineteen in 1901 to twenty-four in 1910.[4] Other evidence, drawn from forty-four towns in Britain and Ireland by the Board of Trade in the early 1900s, invariably shows Norwich workers to be among the very worst off, working the longest hours for the lowest rates of pay.[5] While none of this information precludes the question of renewed trade union growth in terms of numbers or activity before 1914, it undoubtedly points towards low levels of workplace trade union involvement and impact. An examination of those cases where more detail is available confirms this view.

Typically, those disputes which occurred in the early 1900s were of a small and fragmented nature, in which employers held the initiative and trade unions, though attempting to resist, were unable to attract sufficient support to prevent victimisations. The Trades Council, still dominated by the Liberals at this time, made only cautious gestures and was unwilling, or more likely unable, to deliver more than token solidarity actions. Thus when Boulton and Paul, who had previously victimised members of the Amalgamated Society of Engineers and the Carpenters and Joiners, sacked four members of the Amalgamated Society of Mill Sawyers for belonging to that union, the Trades Council's offer to act as a mediator in the dispute was rebuffed.[6] Similarly when three members of the Amalgamated Society of Tramwayworkers were victimised in December 1901 no defence was organised by other workers on the trams. The Trades Council arranged a public meeting and concert on behalf of the men and opened a relief fund to supplement their union's limited benefit pay 'until they obtain employment', but could not secure their re-instatement.[7]

Two disputes in 1905 further illustrate the problems facing local workers, though in these cases the Trades Council could do still less, as most of the workers involved were not even trade union members. In the clothing industry, traditionally poorly organised, the local branch of the Amalgamated Society of Tailors, comprised craftsmen who refused to recruit women workers or male machinists. Working conditions deteriorated further with the extension of mechanisation and an even greater emphasis on piece-work rates.[8] A branch of the Amalgamated Union of Clothiers Operatives had been established before 1900 but had made little headway. Its local Secretary, G. Banham, reckoned that average wages in the industry in Norwich were 'thirty and in some cases forty per cent less' than in

Pete Curran
*An organiser of the Gasworks and
General Labourers Union and a regular
speaker in Norwich*

TRADE UNION ACTIVISTS

Bill Holmes
*One of the leading local activists and a
prominent Norwich ILP member.*

London.[9] When piece-work rates for women machinists at Chamberlain's clothing factory were reduced by almost half in July 1905, thirty of the women struck — though only a handful were union members — without success.[10] There was a similar occurrence at Southall's shoe works that September. Fifty workers, none of them union members, struck in protest at the appointment of a 'notorious' deputy as a foreman, but again unsuccessfully, and five were actually taken to court by the company for not working their week's notice.[11]

Exceptions to this state of affairs were few. In the printing industry the local branch of the Typographical Association had built up to 120 members, out of a total of 300 printworkers in the city, by 1902. While those working on newspapers were paid reasonable rates, the 'fair' fixed wage for the remainder was 26/- per week, which the Association wished to raise to 28/-.[12] When sixty members were called on strike at the end of March 1902 a dispute pattern so often seen in Norwich was re-enacted. Eighteen were immediately offered improved terms before the strike began, but those who did strike were locked out by their employers. After thirteen weeks the strike collapsed. The 28/- wage was not established for several more years, although the union did recruit further, the local branch having 170 members by 1910.[13] A second area of trade union growth at the opening of the 1900s was at Colman Foods, where Bill Holmes and a few other ILP members were involved in building a branch of the Gasworkers and General Labourers Union several hundred strong.[14] But while the employers made concessions and avoided conflict in the departments where the union was known to be entrenched, they also used other tactics. One was to transfer union activists to less well paid jobs, thereby disrupting the union organisation and deterring would-be militants. Another was to maximise employer advantages from changes in work processes, for in 1905 it was reported that, 'A great alteration has taken place in the organisation of work, and new machinery has been introduced with its natural concomitant, the speeding up of human labour'.[15]

In situations like this the task of those who argued for a workplace or industrial orientation for socialists was made still more difficult. Notwithstanding its electoral emphasis, the ILP had begun to exert an influence in some local trade unions. At the workplace level this cannot be quantified, but the growth of ILP representation on the Trades Council is clear enough. G.H. Roberts and G.F. Hipperson were respectively elected as Trades

Council President in 1902 and Secretary in 1906. Thereafter both these offices were regularly held by other ILP members.[16] Though the ILP sought to maximise its influence from such positions, its efforts also to put new life into the Trades Council had to acknowledge the lack of industrial struggles. Consequently the widening of the Trades Council's political horizons was not matched by a similar expansion in the opportunities for industrial intervention. Thus having endorsed G.H. Roberts as Labour Representation Committee Parliamentary Candidate in 1905, the Trades Council worked jointly with the ILP and SDF in preparation for a May Day demonstration, the first for several years, essentially as a platform for Roberts' campaign.[17] Similarly the Trades Council Executive Committee consulted with the ILP and SDF about the presentation of candidates in municipal and Poor Law Guardian elections. The decision to abandon Trades Council meetings at the close of 1905 'in consequence of the (General) Election Campaign in full progress and most delegates . . . engaged in the work' also indicated where priorities lay.[18] Other issues which the Trades Council specifically campaigned upon included land nationalisation, and unemployment, the subject of its 1908 May Day demonstration.[19] When approached by individual unions, for example the Amalgamated Society of Railway Servants in May 1907, the Trades Council did what it could to help.[20] In particular it made a major effort to assist the Women's Trade Union League organise a series of factory gate and street meetings. As a result, when a renewed conflict occurred at Chamberlain's clothing works in 1908, all the women workers who struck were now members of a trade union, the National Federation of Women Workers.[21]

Although the Trades Council was now taking initiatives, the opportunities for a more positive role in industrial disputes became less frequent in Norwich in the years before the war. This was in marked contrast with the national situation.[22] Locally there was no coal-mining industry, while cotton textiles and dock-work were insignificant and engineering was still on a relatively small scale. Thus many of the great 'national' disputes of 1908-13 passed Norwich by, and the suggested 'strike wave' effect seen in other parts of the country did not materialise.[23] The local situation is best illustrated by examining two conflicts which did occur, the city-wide dispute in the shoe industry in 1908 and the strike of agricultural labourers in nearby St Faith's in 1910.

In the shoe industry greater mechanisation and the process of concentration brought both more regular work and technological unemployment. However, '. . . a common theme in the union's Minute Books and Branch Reports was that the limited number of "Society Men" made opposition to wage reducing policies difficult'.[24] Even in the largest firms, where conditions were better and jobs more secure, work patterns and methods of payment were continually being switched by management.[25] Thus it was the very weakness of the Norwich shoe workers and the desire of the national union to improve wages and organisation in the city which account for the dispute of 1908.

In 1907 the union had commenced a recruitment campaign, publicising its desire to 'sort out' Norwich and its willingness to spend up to £100,000 in order to win a minimum wage agreement. On this basis perhaps 1,100 shoe workers were recruited in preparation for a dispute.[26] When the union submitted its claim for a minimum weekly wage of 30/- in January 1908, it expressed its willingness to negotiate on the sum involved only if the principle of the minimum wage was conceded. On the other hand, the employers were prepared solely to discuss levels of pay.[27] An all-Norwich strike was threatened in February, and with large numbers potentially involved the employers could not quickly find sufficient replacement labour. But equally it is unlikely that the National Union of Boot and Shoe Operatives wanted to spend funds on a protracted dispute despite their earlier assertions. Consequently both sides were amenable to a proposal from Louis Tillett, the local Liberal MP, for a joint meeting presided over by the Mayor. This produced proposals for a minimum wage, not of 30/-, but at the 1907 average level of 26/-. Though there would be in-built subsequent pay rises, these amounted only to an additional 1/- in 1910 and in 1911 but with no further rise before 1913.[28]

One result of this settlement was that in the years before 1914 Norwich shoeworkers remained poorly paid, relative to those in other areas, though the minimum wage stimulated the further decline of the worst paid subcontract work. Another was that a key section of the local Labour Movement underwent a further long period of quietude, with only one brief dispute of any size in 1911, and with overall NUBSO membership dropping back to 1,700 by 1914.[29] A third aspect was that while this dispute was large by Norwich standards, the role of the Liberal MP and the Mayor, and the nature of the settlement suggest little in the way of rank and file union activity. Still less were there signs of industrial based politics of a socialist or syndicalist kind, even though the ILP had a presence among local shoe workers. Thus although the historian of the NUBSO suggests 'with this success, boot and shoe unionism in Norwich at last struck roots', the real gains and the level of involvement of ordinary shoe workers were less than might have been assumed.[30]

A glimpse of what could be achieved in terms of mobilising the local Labour Movement was seen in 1910 with the agricultural labourers' disputes in Trunch, Knapton and, particularly relevant to Norwich, St Faith's.[31] In 1906 the Eastern Agricultural Labourers and Smallholders Union had been founded in North Walsham and, though this was seen by many farmworkers as their union, it was very much controlled by the Liberal Party as a vote-gathering machine.[32] By 1907 the union had over 3,000 members, mainly in Norfolk. The few socialists within it began to win support for 'a forward movement' to improve pay and conditions and also for affiliation to the Labour Representation Committee. Such aims, the antithesis of Liberal objectives, were resisted, but in 1909 and 1910 a series of small, unofficial strikes occurred. These culminated in the St Faith's dispute which lasted from May 1910 until February 1911.[33] In this, 105 men struck for 1/- per week extra and for a Saturday half-day. There were soon clashes with blacklegs, involving practically the whole village, and two women and twelve men were arrested and fined.

The strike was a source of embarrassment to the senior Liberal figures on the union's Executive who had no wish to see open class struggle in the countryside, particularly when this coincided with the General Election campaign of 1910. They postponed Executive Committee meetings and blocked constitutional calls for a special general meeting of the union to discuss the strike, before settling the dispute over the heads of the membership. A direct consequence of such behaviour was that thirty-three of the strikers were re-engaged only on the old terms, while four more were left victimised.[34]

This demonstration of the practical value of Liberalism to the Norfolk farmworker contrasted sharply with the efforts of the labourers themselves and with those of the Norwich Trades Council and ILP. The ILP had undertaken propaganda work in Norfolk long before the St Faith's dispute occurred, and some of its members were involved in the Trunch and Knapton disputes.[35] Throughout the St Faith's dispute weekly workplace collections were organised in Norwich, while rural support meetings were held by or assisted by ILP cycling teams.[36] Almost 1,600 agricultural labourers joined the union in the course of the dispute, proof that activity was a better recruiting agent than Liberal panaceas of allotments and smallholdings. And though membership declined after the betrayal of the St Faith's strikers, the political change was irreversible. When the union held its Annual Conference in February 1911, a motion of no confidence in the Executive was moved by ILP members and carried by the delegates. Only one of the union officers who had agreed the St Faith's settlement survived the new elections. Their replacements were almost wholly from those who had participated in or built support for the dispute. Thus, while the ILP neither controlled the union nor monopolised the political loyalties of its membership, it now had a strong influence at the Executive level. It had also made considerable progress in breaking previous allegiances to the Liberal Party and in building closer links between organised labour in Norwich and Norfolk.[37]

The St Faith's episode showed that the Norwich Labour Movement could deliver trade union solidarity and that local socialists were willing to play a leading role. Yet the fact that such abilities were expended in a rural dispute is not without significance. It has been suggested that the ILP and other early socialists looked to rural workers because the agrarian tradition was very much part of their socialism.[37] If this was the case, Norwich socialists, by virtue of their location, would be especially influenced by such traditions.[38] It seems more likely, however, that the attractions of organising rural workers in struggles against Norfolk farmers were enhanced by the absence of opportunities to do likewise in Norwich itself.

This latter feature is illustrated, for example, by events in the course of the national railway strike of 1911. Neither of the railway companies operating in Norwich was a stronghold of trade unionism, and the General Railway Workers Union, which had been prominent in Norwich, was much less of a force on the railways than the Amalgamated Society of Railway Servants by 1900.[39] Thus although there was a Labour or Socialist presence in the ASRS in Norwich in the early 1900s, the extent of its influence at workplace level was questionable. In the 'Hot August' of 1911 the local press reported on the rapid spread of the unofficial railway strike, the onset of the dock and transport strikes in London, the start of the miners' strike in South Wales, and the tramways disputes in Leeds and Glasgow.[40] However, the political and industrial temperature in Norwich remained a good deal lower.[41] When the leaders of the ASRS finally called for an official, national strike on 16 August the only notable local response came from clerks at Norwich Thorpe station, who refused to issue tickets to travellers intending to use the London North Western Railway. Two days later, it was reported that, 'Norwich has to a large extent escaped from the unpleasant consequences attending a stoppage of railway traffic . . . up to now the Great Eastern Railway have daily run their full service of trains'.[42] On the GER, company circulars indicated that 'extra pay would be granted during the strike to those who continued faithful in their duty to the Company'. This was enough to account for all but the most active of trade unionists.[43] On the Midland and Great Northern Joint Railway trade union density was higher, at least one third. Its General Manager noted the workers were '. . . reasonable and conciliatory . . . [but] . . . guarded as to what their decision would be if they received a command from their union. . . .'[44]

At best then, there was uncertainty as to the nature of the strike call, and some indifference. In Norwich there was, 'an active strike committee in the city . . . doing its best to bring the local railwayworkers into line with their fellows elsewhere'.[45] But its influence was limited. When it called an emergency meeting to discuss the strike, fewer than fifty railway workers attended and a resolution to take strike action was carried by just eighteen votes to fifteen, the rest abstaining. It was a result which ensured that the strike call was abandoned.[46] The local press reported that the railway workers 'were obviously desirous of very carefully considering the matter before committing themselves to the course urged upon them by their leaders'.[47] This suggests both a lack of the enthusiasm for the strike seen elsewhere, and insufficient preparation by activists in Norwich, who were caught by the speed at which the dispute spread. It was one thing to win arguments within trade union branch meetings about which Parliamentary candidate to endorse, quite another to overcome the lack of basic organisation and to convince sizeable numbers of workers of the need for strike action.

Considerations of this kind plagued the Labour Movement in Norwich in the years immediately preceding the First World War. Lack of trade union activity is not generally regarded as newsworthy, therefore press sources do not allow the building of a detailed picture of the trade union movement in these years, comparable with that of the early 1890s. But the fragments are suggestive enough. We have already examined the quietude after 1908 in the shoe industry, and in the building trades the story is similar. Nationally it has been suggested, 'The change from conflict to peace coincided with the change from ten years of boom to ten years of depression' in this industry. The recession was reflected in rising unemployment and a decline in trade union membership. There is no evidence to show that building workers in Norwich were immune from these features.[48] Bricklayers, stonemasons, carpenters and joiners, plumbers and plasterers, paid at the agreed craft rate of 8d per hour in 1902, had at best seen no improvement in wages before 1913. Given the fragmented nature of the industry, it is also likely that 'agreed' rates may have in practice been optimum rates in these years. In any event the Norwich rates were lowest or equal lowest of those paid in forty-four towns surveyed by the Board of Trade.[49] Painters similarly remained on rates of 6½d per hour between 1902 and 1913, while plasterers' and bricklayers' labourers, paid nominally 5d per hour, were even more prone to the pressures of under-employment on their wages.[50]

In the city's other main industries, such as clothing and food and drink, trade unions remained very much on the defensive, unable to improve pay or working conditions appreciably. Even in some of the largest workplaces in these sectors the unions had no foothold. The spread of mechanisation in the clothing industry has already been noted. While this produced slightly more regular work, it also undercut skilled rates for men and was of no financial benefit to women on revised piece-work rates.[51] The latter remained largely unorganised despite the efforts of the National Federation of Women Workers, and average factory earnings per week, estimated in 1910 at 10/9d for women and 5/6d for girls, had shown little improvement over the previous five years.[52] Conditions and pay were still worse in sweatshops and retailing. An investigation into 'The Shop Slaves of Norwich' showed women dressmakers aged twenty, having served their two-year apprenticeship, on rates of 8/- to 12/- per week in the busy season, with 'three-quarter' time from September to April.[53] Considering retailing generally, the survey reckoned, 'there is no doubt that the shop assistants are amongst the lowest paid, and work longer hours than any other class of labour in Norwich'.[54] In the food and drink industries, trade unionism had been checked at Colmans, but its continued presence there perhaps partly accounts for the payment of male minimum wages of 21/- per week in 1910, as against a city average in this section of between 16/- and 18/-.[55] Colmans was reckoned one of the better employers: more common was the case of Caleys, the city's principal confectioners, where 'trade unionism is unknown' and a great deal of the pasting, labelling and wrapping was still done on an outworking basis for much lower wages.[56]

Among the more skilled occupations trade unionism seemed stronger, but if comparative wage rates for similar trades elsewhere in the country are any indicator, this strength was illusory. In 'engineering', pattern makers, turners and fitters in Norwich earned 32/- for a fifty-four-hour working week, the lowest rates paid in the forty-four towns surveyed except for Dundee and Aberdeen.[57] In the larger local concerns, such as the Great Eastern Railway, Boulton and Paul and Lawrence and Scott, skilled engineers' wages had crept up towards 34/- by 1910, but 32/- was the normal basic wage in other firms as late as 1914, while semi-skilled wages varied between 20/- and 25/-.[58] Both the Friendly Society of Ironfounders and the Electrical Trades Union had branches in the city, but rates of pay for their members were the lowest among those recorded by the Board of Trade, both in 1902 and in 1914.[59] As Hawkins commented, 'Trade unionism in this section is not strong. Electrical engineers are practically not organised at all. The Amalgamated Society of Engineers musters under 200 members, and the Steam Engine Makers less than 100'.[60] And whereas the strongly organised litho-printers on local newspapers earned some of the best wages paid outside London, the failure of the 1902 strike among lower paid compositors ensured that these remained among the lowest paid in the country.[61]

The prospects of immediate improvement for trade unionists thinly spread in low paid or irregular work such as cartage, furnishings or general labour, were bleak.[62] No doubt there were many potential trade union members here, but they were still to be recruited on the eve of World War One. For the features sometimes seen in other areas, for example the strike wave or the enthusiastic adoption of militant, campaigning trade unionism in one section of industry which then spread to others, were not present in Norwich. Though industrial unrest exploded in Britain at this time, many of the disputes, for example in mining or shipbuilding, had no direct bearing on workers in the city. Others, such as those in the docks, on the railways and other sectors of transport, drew little or no response locally, either because the number of workers directly affected was comparatively small, or because trade union organisation was too weak. In engineering, where the offensive 'strike wave' became a feature in some areas, there was no leading group of workers taking the initiative in Norwich. And in the essentially defensive disputes in the textiles industries, it was the least affected clothing sector which was most in evidence in Norwich.[63] Such 'big battalions' as the Norwich Labour Movement possessed were in the shoe industry, quiet after 1908, and in building, perhaps the one national industry in which trade union activity declined after 1900.

Inter-related with these considerations is the question of political development. The politics of industrial militancy determined that in disputes the struggle should be spread. In advanced form this meant generalising conflict with capitalists. More limited objectives were to put pressure upon a particular employer or to win sympathetic actions from fellow workers. But in the absence of trade union militancy and disputes, such aims were unlikely to attract mass support in Norwich, as they had little else to offer and did not appear to correspond with the situation locally.

None of this is to say that workers in Norwich were unaware of the rise of trade union militancy. Rather, national features were subjected to close appraisal in the light of local experience. Instead the more passive politics of 'Representation' as the realistic option for the local Labour Movement predominated. This compounded further the weakness of workplace organisation and relegated it to a secondary role, notwithstanding the numerical growth of some local trade unions.[64] Such developments were not irreversible, but became pronounced in the Norwich Labour Movement in the years before 1914. And important though it was, the emphasis on vote gathering in the politics of Labour Representation could blur, rather than sharpen, those divisions which open class struggle threw into stark contrast.[65]

6

Liberal and Labour

Labour Representation 1903-1906

Although the economic and legal difficulties which beset trade unions in the early years of the twentieth century stimulated the attractions of Parliamentary representation for the trade union leaderships, the achievements of the Labour Representation Committee were as yet minor. Only Keir Hardie had been elected as a genuine LRC MP in the jingoistic atmosphere of the General Election in 1900, and though he was formally joined by Richard Bell, the latter had by no means broken from Liberalism. Three other LRC candidates returned in by-elections in 1902-3 were also very close to the 'Lib/Lab' outlook. This meant that the base for independent Labour Representation remained qualitatively as well as quantitatively weak.[1] As will be seen, electoral arrangements with the Liberal Party were beginning to be discussed even at this point and, while helping Labour's numbers in Parliament, these were unlikely to aid its development as a separate entity.

However these were unresolved questions, as was the whole issue of 'New Liberalism'. It has been suggested that some erstwhile Liberal supporters, disillusioned by the Party's lack of firm opposition to the South African War and its inability to defend workers' interests, became an additional element in the LRC.[2] Yet developments in this direction were overshadowed by the convergence of Liberal and early Labour opinion in defence of Free Trade and, apparently, on questions of social reform. Again, the full implications of 'New Liberalism' *vis à vis* workers' interests and the ability of a Parliamentary Labour group to force the pace of social reform were not clear. Nationally, then, there was still much promise in Labour Representation.

A third feature of the early 1900s was the rise of interest in municipalisation. While anti-Labour elements overreacted to the extent and progress of municipalisation, there were many who, whether they considered

63

themselves to be Socialist, Labour or Liberal, anticipated a decentralisation of political power. In this they saw the basis for a political alternative and a direct means of improving the condition of the working class, particularly the unorganised. With the widening of the local franchise, here apparently was the opportunity for the practical socialism of Labour Representation to be applied at the local level.[3] Such possibilities were overestimated by many socialists, not least because municipalisation could also be a weapon held in Liberal or Tory hands.[4] It is the local dimensions of these features that are the subject of this chapter.

Support for municipalisation as the instrument of practical politics in Norwich was initially limited. The Independent Labour Party, flushed with success after the School Board elections, had announced its intention of standing a Parliamentary candidate in August 1900 but quickly found the political atmosphere not to its liking and for a second time had to cancel such plans.[5] Similarly the Radical minority again had the chastening experience of seeing local Liberal leaders present the Tories with a walk-over in the October General Election, rather than embarking upon a campaign which would reveal their own divisions. Thus it may be that interest in municipal reform reflected the desire to take a new form of political action which offered the prospect of positive results and also an alternative to swimming against the patriotic tide. The Municipal Reform Union which began to hold meetings in October 1900, comprising delegates from the SDF, ILP, Trades Council and local Radicals, decided to field three candidates in the local elections the next month. However, there was no clear programme apart from a commitment to municipalisation and the payment of trade union rates to municipal employees. The campaign produced disappointing results. Two of the three Municipal Reform Union candidates pulled out of their contests, fearing they might be victimised at work. The third, Scott, was a trade union official supported by Roberts for the ILP and by Henderson for the Radicals. But he failed against the sitting Liberal.[6] The only success for 'Municipalisation' actually came from another direction. Following an upheaval among Ber St ward Liberals, the Fabian H.A. Day was elected in opposition to the sitting Liberal Councillor, W. Goddard.[7]

The very confusions of these elections mark the beginnings of a process of realignments in local politics. The Municipal Reform Union, sustained largely by the SDF and ILP, survived for a time to focus attention on social questions and the Liberals' lack of commitment to municipalisation in practice. For so long as the Liberal understanding of social reform was based essentially upon temperance reform and non-sectarianism in education, there were opportunities for the advocates of wider municipalisation to make inroads upon working-class Liberal supporters. If there was no guarantee that the latter would shift their ground, at least the audiences in the working-men's Radical Clubs in Magdalen Street or Old Palace Road were likely converts.[8] Compared with the clientele at the Liberals' power centre in The Walk or at the Gladstone Club in St Giles', they could respond to issues like the legal Eight Hour Day, work for the unemployed, old age pensions and other state provision for the sick and disabled. Until there was a clearly defined Liberal response, in terms of 'New Liberalism' and municipal reform, support among some of the 'advanced radicals' and Liberal trade union activists could be siphoned off. Potentially this gave the ILP in particular the prospect of an electoral breakthrough. Thus the question of municipalisation became predominant after 1900, developing as an area of common, though very much contested, ground among radicals and socialists.[9]

In 1901 the Norwich ILP ran candidates in both the Guardians' and municipal elections, in itself an indication that the Party was recovering from its doldrums of 1895-8.[10] H.E. Witard, the municipal candidate in Coslany was able to force the sitting Liberal, a landlord who had been served with writs because of the insanitary conditions of some of his properties, on to the defensive. He came within fifty votes of winning the contest. Witard's Municipal Address called for the control of water, gas, telephones and housing, and the erection of 'workmen's dwellings'. He further advocated the enforcement of trade union rates of pay and conditions in all contract work for the City Corporation, an extension of its Direct Works Department and the introduction of the Eight Hour working day.[11] The following year Witard narrowed the difference to twenty-four votes, having campaigned for a detailed programme of municipal reform. This attracted support from the SDF and, more desirable from the ILP viewpoint, the endorsement of H.A. Day, the Liberal councillor, who thereby risked expulsion from Liberal ranks.[12] At the third attempt in 1903 Witard was elected in Coslany ward, following a campaign involving some eighty helpers, which revealed both the importance of electoral effort to the ILP and the value it attached to inflicting a first defeat upon the Liberals.[13]

There was then sufficient interest in municipal reform locally for the ILP to use it as a weapon against the Liberals. Similarly with the SDF: in 1904 W.R. Smith was elected to the Board of Guardians in the Mousehold ward, largely on the SDF advocacy of housing reform.[14]

Municipalisation was also an issue within the local Liberal Party though for varying motives. For the 'advanced radicals' influenced by Fred Henderson municipalisation and socialism were synonymous, with socialism defined somewhat imprecisely, as 'The civic administration of industry as a means of bringing the conditions of life and work under the direct control of the organised social conscience. . . .'[15] Whatever this was, it would spread gradually as municipal control extended. Henderson's immediate aim was to win the Liberal Party over to a Municipal Reform Programme, which he saw as being critical to social improvement and electoral support. His election as a city councillor in the Fye Bridge ward and a series of successful public meetings demonstrated that there were political gains to be made from the issue, and a Municipal Programme was adopted by the Liberals in 1903. In this they announced, 'We stand as a Party for the public ownership and control of all those services which are essential to the public health and convenience. . . .' They referred specifically to lighting, tramways and water, 'an efficient housing scheme' and the payment of trade union rates to public employees.[16]

Yet while Henderson was seen as a socialist by Liberal officials, he was also regarded as their ally against the ILP. Thus, in April 1903, he was arguing, 'There was one section of socialists, represented by the ILP, who took the view that the relationship between Liberalism and Socialism must necessarily be a hostile one . . . it was a short-sighted view . . . the simple fact was that Liberalism in England today stood for collectivism to an extent that even its own leaders had not yet recognised'.[17] Such views were endorsed by dominant local Liberal figures who saw municipalisation as an accompaniment to national social reform and a means of attracting and holding working class support. As Councillor Keefe told Wensum ward Liberals, 'It was only to the Liberal Party that they could look for such legislation. Fully granting the honesty and earnestness of independent or sectional action, such action could not secure the important reforms which were essential to the labour programme'.[18] It was this strategy, of blocking municipal schemes on the grounds of economy rather than principled opposition, which was employed by the effective leader of the local

Liberals, Louis Tillett, between 1903 and 1906. This was to prove a decisive factor in Henderson's break with the Liberals in 1906. In fact leading Liberals demonstrated a much greater grasp of the uses of the municipalisation issue than Henderson gave them credit for, and they were quite content to allow him to add a radical gloss to their local themes.[19]

By 1903 then municipal reform was already a major question in Norwich. Both the ILP and SDF had made gains from it, but so too had the Liberals, and that Party's loss to the ILP of one council seat in the 1903 elections was more than compensated by gains from the Tories. All told, the Liberals had increased their majority over the Conservatives to seven in 1903. Opposition to the Conservatives' 1902 Education Act, which had abolished the elected School Boards, was likely to have been a feature in these results, given strong Nonconformist traditions in Norwich. But while acknowledging this, Henderson ascribed the outcome to his Municipal Reform programme, arguing, 'First and foremost it is due to the fact that the Liberal Party was not fighting for mere party stake, but for a defined and explicit policy in municipal affairs'.[20] As the Liberal leaders would undoubtedly have said, he was entitled to his opinion.

None of this is to suggest that local Liberal figures were any more in control of the destiny of the Labour Movement in Norwich than were Henderson or the ILP. Yet from around 1900 onwards, Party efforts to influence the movement were increasing, and national considerations in particular became dominant. Though there remained scope for local emphasis, and sometimes even resistance, the tendency was for grass-roots members to have much less control over decision making than their ability to participate indicated. While there is evidence for this at the level of municipal affairs, the development was most marked in the representation of labour interests at the national level and, above all, in the years 1903-06 when the arrangements of the 'MacDonald - Gladstone Entente' were brought to bear on a largely unsuspecting electorate and upon local party organisations.[21]

Briefly, the immediate national background was that even in its first year of existence the LRC was investigating the possibilities of avoiding direct confrontations with the Liberal Party in General Elections. If necessary, this included the LRC adopting the role of 'junior partner'. A sub-committee of Ramsay MacDonald and Edward Pease, examining local opportunities, pinpointed double-seat constituencies for a tactical arrangement whereby one Labour and one Liberal MP might be elected. Norwich was one such constituency, and an arrangement with the Liberals was ratified by the LRC Executive in January 1901. This was precursor to the national arrangement of 1903 whereby eleven double-seat constituencies were targeted for the 'One plus One' system, with Labour being unopposed by the Liberals in thirty single-seat constituencies and giving the Liberals a free hand in the remainder.[22]

Yet the course of events and the conduct of the leading political figures in Norwich suggest that initially few were aware of these arrangements and, of those that were, most kept silent while others showed an inclination not to fall into line. In September 1900 the Norwich ILP announced its intention of standing its own candidate in the forthcoming General Election, before the Liberals had made their views known. Though this election campaign was abandoned, the signs were that the ILP was carefully preparing the ground. In June 1900 two ILP members, Roberts and Lund, had persuaded the Norwich Trades Council Executive Committee to contact the LRC, although the ILP had already announced Roberts' candidature by this point.[23] Yet the question of affiliation to the LRC by the Trades Council was not approved until June 1901. And the conference 'representing trade unionists, co-operators, social democrats and the ILP', which formally drew up plans for Labour Representation, did not take place until September 1901.[24]

Such a drawn-out timetable indicates the degree of political stonewalling and manoeuvring involved, even allowing due time for consideration of financial and other arrangements. Among the advocates of Labour Representation the ILP's choice of G.H. Roberts was not universally approved. In a campaign apparently orchestrated by Henderson, many of the dissenters turned up at the special meeting of the Norwich Co-operative Society which refused to endorse Roberts and pulled out of the local Labour Representation scheme.[25] Within the Liberal Party few felt that Roberts, judging from their differences in the School Board elections, was close to them. Some argued that the ILP was moving too quickly, while others expressed outright opposition to the very principle of separate Labour Representation. And in Norwich ILP itself there were suspicions of Roberts' ambitions and ability, though moves to adopt Pete Curran of the Gasworkers Union instead were frustrated by Curran's prior selection as Parliamentary candidate for Jarrow.[26] Doubtless pleased by Roberts' apparent lack of success, the Editor of *Daylight* noted that the trade union response to the Labour Representation levy had so far been poor, with many trade unionists objecting to the use of funds for 'political' purposes. He concluded, 'The impression prevails largely about the city that the Trades Council proposal was being carefully engineered by a small Roberts clique in order to foist that incapable person upon the city as a Labour Candidate'.[27] If the ILP was trying to do its job, Liberal trade unionists and others were also attempting to do theirs.

While it is impossible to measure the extent of personal animosity to Roberts against the question of separate Labour Representation, the evidence cited suggests that early in 1902 very few people were familiar with the LRC/Liberal arrangements. If the common interest of Radicals and Socialists in municipalisation and social reform was giving rise to some thought of co-operation, this was not slanted towards Parliamentary campaigns.[28] Moreover, in 1902 the Norwich Liberals were in some disorder. While aware that the ILP was trying to build up momentum for its candidate, they had as yet named none of their own. Until Louis Tillett became an authoritative figure, Norwich Liberals relied upon an 'honorary leader', George White, the MP for West Norfolk, while the Council group was led by the elderly Alderman Dakin. Both men were Gladstonians.[29] Thus it was a complete surprise when, in September 1902, White announced that he favoured the principle of direct Labour Representation in Parliament and '. . . made a direct recommendation to the Liberal Executive Committee . . . that they should consider the possibility of adding one to the class of members he had described.'[30]

White having raised the 'possibility' of a direct Labour candidate - he did not suggest one from outside the ranks of the Liberals - it was left to another Gladstonian mouthpiece, the *Eastern Daily Press* to prepare the electorate for this next step. A suitable occasion was the municipal election in Fye Bridge ward where Henderson, on close terms with the Liberals and no friend to the ILP was standing as 'Progressive' candidate. The Liberal Party publicly supported Henderson, and the *EDP* enthused, 'The spectacle of Labour fighting Liberal candidates . . . or Liberals fighting Labour men, is a pitiful one for all of us who have the cause of the poor really at heart. We are glad that in Fye Bridge so excellent an example of Progressive unity is being set'.[31] Yet by the year end there was still no public statement as to Liberal intentions. It was clear that Roberts would be Parliamentary candidate of the ILP, if not the LRC, and that Tillett would be "one" Liberal candidate.[32]

When Roberts was formally selected as ILP candidate at a meeting addressed by Hardie in February 1903, he was supported by three Liberal councillors, Day, Barker and Rev. Stone. They were still campaigning for the Liberal Party to accept a Labour nominee as its second candidate and apparently had no knowledge of the 1901 or 1903 electoral arrangements.[33] By now the ILP effort was fully under way, with more trade union endorsements for Roberts than in the previous year.[34] In contrast, the Liberal caucus meeting which formally adopted Tillett as sole Liberal representative was a tame affair. Alderman White merely informed the local membership that as Roberts was already running they would stand only one candidate 'that they might not complicate the position'.[35]

What greatly complicated the position was the death of Sir Harry Bullard, one of the sitting Tory MPs. This necessitated a Parliamentary by-election, not considered under the terms of the MacDonald/Gladstone Entente, in January 1904. As in previous municipal contests, the straight fight between ILP and Liberals for the 'Progressive' vote led to several switches of allegiance and much bitterness. Both Roberts and Tillett were endorsed by the TUC Parliamentary Committee, both exploited the themes of Free Trade, the excesses of the South African War, and the Nonconformist opposition to the Conservatives' Education Act. However, local newspapers sympathetic to such views presented Roberts as an 'uncompromising socialist', who nevertheless had his 'duty as a Free Trader to retire and leave the field clear'.[36] While Liberal speeches centred upon Free Trade, their election leaflets were full of spoiling slogans, 'A vote for Roberts is a wasted vote', 'Roberts cannot win', and 'The ILP is trying to destroy the chances of a Progressive victory'.[37] For its part, the ILP was able to secure the backing of a number of Liberal councillors, notably Day and Crotch.[38] Yet a number of local advocates of Labour Representation, particularly Henderson and his supporters, refused to endorse Roberts, and many national ILP and LRC figures were far from keen on this direct challenge to the Liberals.[39]

In the election Roberts, with 2,444 votes, trailed a poor third behind the victorious Tillett (8,576 votes) and the Protectionist Tory, Ernest Wild (6,757 votes).[40] This result demonstrated that the ILP had still to make an electoral breakthrough, and that its trade union base was too weak to transform official endorsements into members' votes. Yet it should also be stressed that the ILP had to fight not only Liberals and Tories, but also many of the 'advanced Radicals' and those broadly in favour of Labour Representation. Arguing that the ILP had an insufficient base from which to challenge the Liberals, Henderson did all he could to maximise the Liberal vote. In letters to an eager Liberal press he wrote, for example, 'The ILP has no more right to describe itself as the Labour movement than any other score or so of irresponsible and unrepresentative persons, coming together as an association'. He also attempted to establish a Norwich Labour League, 'For Labour men . . . not prepared to swallow a dose of socialism with their Labour principles'.[41] Not until 1905 did Henderson publicly reveal that his behaviour and that of like-minded Radicals was linked to a longer term plan. Their votes had '. . . transferred from Mr Roberts to Mr Tillett on the explicit understanding that in return for them the Liberal Party would support Mr Roberts at the General Election'.[42] This suggests either that Henderson knew something of the national 'Entente', or that local Liberal leaders had granted as a 'concession' to Radicals in 1904 the national arrangements already made in 1903, or even 1901. In this light the ILP vote, which was not in any case insignificant for a first effort, was the 'hard' vote of those enticed by neither the Liberals nor the sophistry of other alleged proponents of separate Labour Representation. Moreover, the ILP was able to recruit out of the campaign. Over thirty new members joined in January 1904 and a further seventy in the next two months according to the Branch Secretary, who informed *Daylight* that his '. . . organisation was never so strong numerically or financially as it is today'.[43] Thus, although the Liberals had their triumph in 1904, the ILP performance was more impressive than first sight would indicate.

Meanwhile, the Norwich Liberals were able to combine an official announcement of the Entente with an apparently generous gesture, resolving in the next General Election, 'To leave open the second seat in the hope that it will be contested in the interests of Progressive political thought and Free Trade by a representative of Labour.[44] Yet such efforts to prepare the ground for the 'One plus One' electoral arrangements were not well received within the ranks of Norwich Liberals. The Caucus which sanctioned the official strategy also called upon local trade unions to send delegations to a special meeting, at which a Labour candidate with whom the Liberals could co-operate would be selected.[45] Liberal hopes that an ILP member such as G.H. Roberts could be pushed out of consideration as Labour Parliamentary candidate were paralleled by trade union concern that Roberts' appointment as Southern Area Organiser for the Typographical Association would make him too remote from the local political scene.[46] And in the municipal elections in 1904 the Liberals were able to blunt the ILP offensive in the Coslany ward by standing a trade unionist of their own. Success here prompted renewed demands for a second Liberal Parliamentary candidate.[47]

Therefore when the Executive of the LRC endorsed Roberts as Labour candidate in January 1908, Liberal and Radical disagreements sharpened. Henderson, with the backing of five Liberal councillors, began to urge all Liberals to support Roberts, stressing that he was now the Parliamentary candidate of Labour rather than of the ILP. But Liberal opponents, with an eye to local influences, publicly began to ask why 'Norwich' should be dictated to by a committee meeting in Liverpool.[48] Meanwhile Norwich ILP launched its own newspaper, geared to the coming General Election, and prematurely began Roberts' election campaign in May 1905.[49] This activity, and rumours that the local Tories were to field only one Parliamentary candidate, exacerbated Liberal fears that their own candidate might be squeezed out by the 'plumping' of Labour or Tory voters.[50] Finally, in the Municipal contests of 1905, the ILP stood three candidates, all against the Liberals. They also took a second seat in Coslany ward where Bill Holmes, now ILP Political Agent and perhaps the fiercest local critic of Liberalism, defeated the sitting Liberal in a straight fight.[51] While the Liberals could do little to stop such ILP initiatives there was a reaction against Henderson, who failed to secure re-election on a 'Progressive' ticket in Fye Bridge ward against a Tory opponent. The local Liberal Association now refused to support him, on the grounds that his advocacy of municipal reform and Labour Representation had 'forced the pace too much in three years'. It was now that Henderson responded by revealing the details of the local arrangement with Liberal leaders in the 1904 by-election.[52]

None of this augured well for an uneventful working of the Entente. Yet in the final months before the General Election of 1906 both Liberal and Labour voters were systematically encouraged by their local party leaders to vote for the 'One plus One' formulation. Once the municipal elections were out of the way the Liberal Executive attempted to quieten dissent by making a public appeal to their supporters. They expressed the hope that,

'... such active steps may be taken as will ensure the return of Messrs Tillett and Roberts, and thus promote the maintenance of Free Trade and the success of Progressive Principles'.[53] With great regularity, the Liberal *Eastern Daily Press* stressed the common ground of free trade. social reform, educational opportunity and support for a Trades Disputes Bill that Liberals and Socialists shared. Its 'Local Topics' section, written by Henderson, practically led readers by the nose. In a single week, for example, the paper referred to '... the determination of the great majority of both Liberal and Labour men in Norwich not to plump in the coming election, but to vote for Tillett and Roberts.' It reassured Liberal waverers that there was 'a note of reality about these Labour meetings', that talk of not supporting Roberts 'has now happily died out' and that 'once attention is focused upon immediate measures... the differences between Liberalism and Labour dissolve away'.[54]

With the beginning of election rallies, the differences between the Liberals and Labour were certainly well concealed by both sides. The *Eastern Daily Press* pointedly informed readers that 'Mr Roberts is LRC candidate and by the constitution of the LRC he cannot definitely associate himself with either the Liberal or the Conservative Party... but he can and does indicate the measures on behalf of which Labour men should use their second vote'.[55] And for his part, Roberts indeed told Labour election audiences that they would, '... take a hand in the return of two members for the city ... we are prepared to carry on the fight against the protectionist policies of Mr Wild ... Norwich electors must show that they are not credulous enough as to return a supporter of the late Government'.[56] Meanwhile Henderson was mending his own fences with the Liberals, apparently concentrating upon mobilising second votes for the LRC. Neither offering nor being invited to speak on Labour platforms, he declared that he now supported a Liberal government, because it would include 'new men, inspired by the modern spirit and in touch with modern thought'. He was on hand at the main Liberal election rally to move the vote of thanks to Tillett, adding, 'They had not only to see that Mr Tillett was returned ... they were going to give their second vote to Mr Roberts [hear, hear] who was with them against Protection, with them on Education ... on all political reforms ... their difference with Mr Roberts was only in degree'.[57] Thus, when Keir Hardie sounded a discordant note in the campaign by expressing 'neither care nor concern' about Labour supporters' use of their second vote, both Henderson and Roberts went out of their way to smooth ruffled feathers. Now it was Henderson's turn to play the local card, suggesting, 'It is his [Hardie's] business to present the Labour case in its national aspect . . . he is not in touch with local circumstances, it is for local people to judge about them'.[58]

The election result in Norwich was hailed as a triumph for Labour. On a massive 92% turnout, Roberts topped the poll with 11,059 votes; Tillett was also elected with 10,972 votes, whilst Wild came a poor third with 7,460. Yet, equally, the result was testimony to the workings of party machines and the Liberal press. Despite the misgivings of many Liberal and Labour supporters, apparent throughout 1905, over ten thousand people voted for the 'One plus One' arrangement of the Entente. The number 'plumping' for one or other of the successful candidates was insignificant.[59]

Though there had been an apparently significant shift within the electorate towards Labour, it was through electoral arrangement with the Liberals that the notionally independent Labour representative became an MP. Roberts was not returned in Norwich on the basis of a rising tide of trade unionism, or a great surge of confidence in independent working-class or socialist organisation. His victory was not even the consequence of a straight political fight with Liberalism. Thus, while the ILP could claim Roberts as 'their man', he was not elected as an ILP candidate and it was clear, not least to Roberts himself, that he would depend upon Liberal support for the foreseeable future. Sympathetic elements within the Liberal Party had helped to return a 'Labour' representative, but not according to their previous strategy of forcing the Liberal Party *en masse* to select and elect working class Liberal candidates. In defeating the Conservatives, the Entente had served its primary purpose for the Liberal leaders; but the blurring of political differences between Liberal and Labour was not to their detriment either. Such developments were to have very different consequences for those who advocated forms of Socialism from below, or who sought to encourage the confidence and ability of local workers to organise for themselves.[60]

7

Making Headway?
Labour Representation 1906-13

Previous chapters have suggested that the trade union arm of the Labour Movement in Norwich was relatively weak in the early 1900s and that the Parliamentary election result of 1906 was less of a breakthrough for the Labour Representation Committee or the Independent Labour Party than a first glance at the voting figures might indicate.[1] Nevertheless there was an undoubted groundswell of support for Labour Representation in the city in the years before World War One. Any examination of this must acknowledge the impetus derived from the events of 1906, and before then the beginnings of a Labour presence on the City Council and the local Board of Guardians. Secondly, the steady development in Norwich of the 'political' arm of Labour was not to be expected in a period which, nationally, saw the emergence of a harder, protectionist Conservatism after the Liberal 'landslide' of 1906, and then an alleged Liberal revival after 1910 which, some historians argue, actually 'contained' Labour.[2]

How can the impact of Labour Representation be assessed? Given Labour's predilection for electoral contests, simple voting figures in local and Parliamentary elections offer one direct line of enquiry. Affected by national political trends, Labour was attempting to make headway in the face of additional local difficulties involving the rise of the Conservatives as the ruling group on the City Council and an emergent Tory/Liberal defensive alliance in municipal contests.[3] Parliamentary elections continued to pose the problem of unravelling solid support for Labour candidates from the tactical voting of Liberals, while an unknown but sizeable number of genuine Labour adherents remained disenfranchised.

If poll counts are less straightforward than they seem, an evaluation of Labour's achievements is even more problematic. What could elected Labour representatives deliver in terms of measures affecting the lives of their supporters? While recognising that the existence of Labour members on local government bodies would mainly be of propagandistic or educational value, the search for material results of what was supposedly practical socialism is surely not an inappropriate exercise. The industrial dimension also has to be considered. In some areas, high levels of industrial conflict often signified the by-passing of electoral processes by workers in favour of the self or class assertions of direct action.[4] In others, industrial struggle added fire to electoral contests, and trade union strength provided weight for Labour's political representatives. Deficiencies in these features would be a hidden yet important feature in Labour Representation in Norwich before 1914. The analysis is therefore confined to the less volatile ground of electoral contests up to 1910 in this chapter, with the immediate pre-World War One years and a wider assessment in the next.

In immediate terms the boost which the ILP received from the 1906 election campaigning was the recruitment of ninety-three new members and a sustained series of street meetings for at least six months afterwards.[5] Although the Norwich Trades and Labour Council was now the official expression of Labour Representation locally, individuals could not join the LRC directly so the ILP was in an ideal position to benefit from the wave of enthusiasm which followed Roberts' election. Over the next few years, however, the picture became much more complex. For while the ILP contested local council and Guardians' elections with renewed vigour, establishing grouplets of three or four members on each body between 1906 and 1912, it was apparently unable to break out from this position. Yet the situation was not stagnant for, as can be seen from Table 1 below, the ILP was able to win seats in new wards, though such gains usually served only to offset the loss of previously held territory. Not until 1909 did the ILP begin to hold on to seats in wards it had won, thereby establishing a firm basis for subsequent growth in the numbers of 'Labour', almost invariably ILP, councillors.

In the period under discussion the composition of the City Council, excluding Aldermen, changed from 24 Liberals, 21 Conservatives, and 3 Labour in 1906, to 25 Conservatives, 17 Liberals and 6 Labour in 1913, with the Tories becoming the ruling group in 1907.[7] A year later they had a peak majority of sixteen over the Liberals and still enjoyed a majority of twelve over both Liberals and Labour in 1909. Furthermore, on some of the great national political issues of these years Free Trade, Home Rule and the

People's Budget Labour was the junior partner in Liberal campaigns against the Conservatives, and these questions obviously had some impact upon municipal voting. More directly, there was the aspect of local Liberal and Conservative collusion against Labour's municipal influence and aspirations. While Liberal and Tory leaders locally never commented openly upon ILP allegations concerning their defensive alliance, from 1908 onwards ILP municipal candidates invariably found themselves opposed by a solitary Liberal or Tory. This seems to point to more than chance happenings or aberrations in the workings of a 'Progressive alliance'. Thus the ILP was attempting to make headway in very disadvantageous circumstances and without the momentum that might be derived from industrial struggles.

Table 1
Wards electing ILP candidates
in Norwich municipal contests 1903-13[6]

	1903	'04	'05	'06	'07	'08	'09	'10	'11	'12	'13
Coslany(1)	+	+	+	-	-	+	+	+	+	+	+
Coslany(2)		+	+	-	-	-	-	-	-	-	
Fye Bridge				+	+	+	-	-	-	-	-
Mousehold(1)				+*	+	+	+	+	+	+	+
Mousehold(2)						+	+	+	-	-	-
Catton(1)					+	+	+	-	-	+	+
Wensum								+	+	+	+
Catton(2)											+
Heigham											+
Total 'Labour' Councillors	1	1	2	3	4	5**	4	3	3	4	6

Key   + won or held

                - lost

                * Mousehold won by 'Socialist and T.U Candidate' 1906

               ** in 1908 H.A.Day, the defecting Liberal, temporarily raised the number of Labour councillors to six.

With two councillors already in Coslany ward, the ILP stood four candidates in municipal elections in the autumn of 1906. It would be dangerous to attach too much weight to the voting figures, but the four polled an average of just over 400 votes each, compared with an average of 320 for the three candidates in 1905. With a seat lost to the Liberals in Coslany and one won from them in Fye Bridge, there was no electoral breakthrough for the ILP though it made other gains.[8] First, W.R. Smith, who successfully stood as 'Socialist and Trade Union' candidate in Mousehold ward with the backing of the Trades Council and SDF, now joined the ILP, becoming its third councillor. Second, Henderson, still an influential figure amongst local Radicals and a prominent supporter of the LRC, and until this time a noted critic of the ILP, broke with the Liberals.

As the recognised architect of the Liberal's Municipal Reform Programme, Henderson wrote a series of letters to the local press in September 1906, castigating the 'municipal parsimony' of Norwich Liberals. He pointed out that while his aim had always been to collaborate 'till we have worked out the great reforms upon which we are both agreed', there was now 'little mileage' in such a venture.[9] The Liberals had dragged their feet on the provision of a municipal water supply and house building and had blocked plans by Henderson, who was supported by the ILP councillors, for a municipal milk supply. He now asked, 'What are many Liberals doing but muddling along in a sympathetic mood without any clear direction in their movement? ... they are looking for a remedy within the existing industrial order and it is the existing industrial order which is the evil'.[10] Henderson stood as 'Socialist' candidate in Lakenham ward, though he failed to beat the sitting Liberal, Crotch, himself a former socialist.[11] He was still not connected with the ILP and the fact that the ILP did not help his election campaign attracted press comment.[12] Yet whatever suspicions may have arisen as to Henderson's ambitions or motives, there is little doubt that, given his record on the municipal question, his action now was a crucial factor for the two parties in their efforts to attract workers' support.

In its relations with a third party, the SDF, there is also evidence that the ILP was gaining the upper hand. Sharing a similar electoral emphasis and producing its own journal, the SDF in Norwich had fewer members than the ILP but was still a contender for workers' allegiance.[13] It began to nominate supporters in Poor Law Guardians' elections in 1901, with one success in Mousehold ward in 1904, and ran its first municipal candidate in Heigham

Making headway?

ward in 1906. Similarly, it had virtually matched the ILP in holding street meetings throughout the latter's recruitment drive of 1905. Moreover, it was still capable of drawing sizeable working class audiences to its major public meetings.[14] For example, H.M. Hyndman spoke on 'Imperialism or Socialism' in November 1905 to an assembly which ... 'In number and intelligence could not have been secured ten years ago ... composed almost exclusively of working men and women, and perhaps the only man on the platform not accustomed to actual manual labour was the lecturer himself'.[15] Lastly, the SDF had a degree of influence within the Trades Council, with which it worked jointly to arrange May Day demonstrations and electoral interventions. Hence Smith's candidature, significantly as 'Socialist and Trade Union' rather than 'Labour', in 1904, or the arrangement in the Guardians' elections in 1907 whereby eight candidates, four ILP, two SDF and two Trades Council were put forward in a united effort.[16]

Despite such co-operation, the ILP resented SDF accusations that the socialist content of the ILP's politics was inevitably being diluted in the Labour Representation Committee. This criticism had been public even before the SDF had withdrawn from the LRC in 1901. But it was used in July 1907 by Norwich ILP as a pretext for blocking joint municipal initiatives along the lines of the arrangements for the Guardians' elections. Proposals for a specific ILP/Trades Council campaign were received by the latter's Executive Committee on 18 July and eventually accepted on 2 September, with the result that SDF candidates in local contests were officially on their own.[17] Whatever its motives in freezing out the SDF, the ILP in Norwich now had a virtual monopoly of socialist representation on both City Council and local Board of Guardians.

A much more serious threat to the ILP came in the shape of a frontal assault by the Conservative Party in the municipal elections of 1907. At precisely the point where the ILP might have expected a boost from Parliamentary by-election victories for socialists in Jarrow and Colne Valley, it was instead an issue arising from the Kirkdale by-election which dominated. In Kirkdale, where religious sectarianism was a major feature, the Conservatives had issued a leaflet quoting an article in *The Clarion* by Robert Blatchford which denounced Christianity.[18] To Conservatives in Norwich it mattered little that Blatchford was not a member of the ILP, nor that the local ILP had more than a sprinkling of ministers of religion in its ranks.[19] Tory defenders of Faith and the Family launched hysterical attacks on the ILP's five candidates. Their standard election leaflet proclaimed: 'Broadly speaking, socialism demands . . . the destruction of home life, the separation of mother from child and the negation of God'.[20] Embellishments on this theme varied, including assertions that socialism was an extreme version of workhouse life and that people would be compelled to live in 'gigantic barracks' in socialist society.[21]

Faced with attacks of this kind, the ILP countered with leaflets on the question of the municipal milk supply for children, which the Tories had refused to support, and on 'Socialism and Free Love', in addition to its usual coverage of municipal issues. How effective these were is difficult to ascertain. The average vote per ILP candidate rose to almost 500, although the new ILP candidate in Coslany failed to hold the ward against a Conservative challenge. Two ward seats were won by the ILP, interestingly in Catton ward by H. Cadman, a father of four and a bandmaster, and in Mousehold ward, gained by temperance advocate and lay preacher, F. Easton.[22] If the personal qualities of the candidates were a factor in the results, the conclusion must be that the ILP overall had been forced on to the defensive.[23] Its post-election meeting reflected this, for members were offered a rather lame excuse and counselled in moderation. W.R. Smith, the Election Agent, explained: 'It was not well that they should increase at too great a rate . . . they must guard against all extravagances of speech and win the confidence of the people of Norwich'.[24] As in the previous year, however, there remained an unexpected bonus for the ILP. H.A. Day, a Norwich manufacturer and consecutively a Liberal, a Fabian, and a supporter of the LRC, maintained his individual progress. Nominated by the Liberals as their candidate in Ber Street, he was elected and then announced his decision to join the ILP.[25].

Thus by the beginning of 1908 three well-known figures associated with the Labour Movement in local politics, Smith, Henderson and Day, had moved to the ILP. At this level the ILP was becoming the pole of attraction and able to speak for the wider Labour Movement. Yet the very speed with which the three newcomers assumed leading positions within the local organisation suggests both the sponge-like qualities of the ILP and the subordination of all else to the electoral effort. ILP members continued to work within the unions and to exert their influence upon the Trades Council primarily in order to make it part of the machinery for contesting elections in the Labour interest. While this involved fighting Liberals as well as

Conservatives at the local level, the class struggle aspects of such activity were limited, especially as General Election arrangements with the Liberals remained intact and the Norwich ILP deliberately distanced itself from the SDF.[26]

A factor which may have sustained those ILP members concerned with such developments was that the Liberals had now effectively, if not openly, combined with the Conservatives in municipal elections to shut out ILP influence. During a Guardians' by-election in Catton in May 1908 the ILP, with a Guardian member already in this ward, was surprised to find that its opposition consisted not of a replacement for the retiring Tory but a solitary Liberal. Despite polling 428 votes in what was a minor contest, the ILP candidate was convincingly beaten.[27] In the November municipal elections, in which the Conservatives continued to make gains from the Liberals, four of the six ILP candidates found themselves facing Tory opponents in wards where the Liberals traditionally had a presence. All four were beaten, despite polling very respectable totals.[28] Only in Coslany ward, where Henderson now stood for the ILP against the sitting Liberal, was there a success. For the second successive year an ILP post-election meeting was warned not to expect easy victories. This time it was Henderson who pointed out that, '. . . they had finally driven their enemies into one camp . . . they now had to fight a combination of the Liberal and Conservative capitalist parties allied against the Socialist movement'.[29]

This situation continued throughout 1909 and 1910, with more evidence to support Henderson's contention. In its fourteenth Annual Report Norwich ILP claimed to have held some 200 public meetings and to have recruited 200 'financial members' over the year. In March 1909 Keir Hardie was able to address one of the largest political meetings ever held in the city, *Daylight* referring to 'the amazing growth in numbers and influence of the supporters of Mr Roberts'.[30] Yet this heralded no change in the Labour representation on the local council. All five ILP candidates in municipal elections were involved in straight fights, the majority against Conservatives, with only one success and a net loss of two seats despite an increased overall vote.[31] With Tory dominance on the City Council now at its height, the reduced group of ILP members also found themselves shut out from representation on council committees. This grievance became one of the ILP's main themes in 1910, the year of two General Elections.[32] Lib/Lab arrangements for the latter did not affect the conduct of the intervening municipal contests, though financial constraints may well explain the ILP decision to put up only three candidates in these. Once again there were disappointments, with defeats at the hands of the Liberals in Catton and Mousehold wards, although H.E. Witard became the first ILP candidate to be elected for Wensum ward and, portentously, to defeat a Tory opponent in three years.[33]

Up to 1910 then, those who favoured Labour Representation in Norwich experienced difficulty in making headway against a revived Conservative Party. Whether this implies Labour had been 'contained', is another matter.[34] The ILP was able to maintain its bridgehead on locally elected bodies and, if not always increasing its total vote, had tended to raise its average vote per candidate. Combined votes of nearly 2,500 and almost 2,900 in five municipal ward elections in 1908 and 1909 compared well with the total ILP vote of some 2,400, attained on a higher turnout in the Parliamentary by-election of 1904. These were reasonable achievements allowing for the need to contest new wards and to establish a core vote in each. Moreover, they occurred in the face of combined manoeuvres by the Conservative and Liberal Parties to minimise ILP influence. Thus, while there is insufficient evidence to show either the precise size of ILP membership or the extent of its influence in the wider Labour Movement locally, it was clearly felt to have consolidated its position since 1906.[35]

While more complex questions concerning the nature of the Labour influence and its local achievements are discussed in chapter eight, the 1910 General Election campaigns in Norwich suggest signs of Labour's further progress.[36] At the time of the Keir Hardie meeting in March 1909, the LRC was sufficiently popular to cause *Daylight* to indulge in new speculations. Roberts had relied heavily upon Liberal votes in 1906, but might he now be able to hold the seat without the need of Liberal assistance? The question required no urgent answer for at the beginning of April 1909 the leader of Norwich Liberals, Edward Copeman, announced their intention of standing a solitary candidate, Frederick Low QC, in a future General Election. Within two months, however, Copeman was revamping the arguments of 1906, explaining to local Liberals '. . . they must remember they had not only to return Mr Low, but they had to keep out a Tory'.[37]

Though nationally the preparations for a continuation of the Lib/Lab Entente were less deliberate than in 1906, the situation in Norwich had already persuaded the Liberals to adopt a cautious approach. They were faced with a revitalised Conservative organisation with a run of municipal successes to its credit and now standing two Parliamentary candidates, including the former MP, Sir Samuel Hoare.[38] While this clearly also posed a threat to Labour, the Liberals appreciated the strength of Roberts' position, and an attempt to maintain an existing 'Progressive, Free Trade' status quo probably represented their safest option.[39] Roberts himself had criticised aspects of the Liberal social reform measures, particularly the pauper disqualification clauses in the 1908 Old Age Pensions Act, but had done little to cause the Liberals offence. At his annual address to constituents in 1909, for example, he had focused upon the problems of tariff reform, indicating its consequences in terms of dear food and unemployment, without discussing living standards or employment levels over the period of Liberal Government.[40]

Consequently the General Election campaign in Norwich in January 1910, in terms of the Lib/Lab voting arrangement, was very much a reworking of 1906 with, if anything, even greater emphasis upon harmony in the face of the great bogeys of Tory protectionism and the Lords' veto. Labour held a series of meetings dealing with Free Trade, the Old Age Pensions and Childrens Acts, and the need for land reform, but when asked about the major issues and the use of second votes Roberts was reported as saying: 'The Labour Party wanted to see the Peers' supporters and the food taxers thoroughly beaten . . . [they] . . . wanted their own man in and also the other candidate who stood for popular representation and for measures of social reform'.[41] At the Liberals' main election rally Low was equally complimentary, although not quite as direct as Roberts. Having concentrated upon the Lords and Free Trade, he went on to announce that he had just read *The ABC of Socialism* by Fred Henderson, 'a man from whom many of them had differed, but they all respected [cheers]'. Low's view was that while socialism 'had a point', it was an ideal only, and in any case 'its time was not yet'.[42]

Even allowing for the fact that in Norwich the industrial base was not as directly threatened by the products of 'Herr Dumper' as in some cities, and that the Liberal attack upon Tory landed privileges might prove particularly popular, the election result was a convincing vindication of the 'One plus One' arrangement. On a 92% turnout, Low topped the poll for the Liberals with 11,257 votes, followed very closely by Roberts with 11,119. The Conservative vote had improved more on the 1906 position, but Hoare

(8,410) and Snowden (7,981) still lagged well behind, their total votes representing only 42% of those cast.[43]

It may be that the Tory strategy of standing two candidates had served to strengthen the Lib/Lab arrangement, for no less than 95% of Liberal and 96% of Labour votes were cast on the 'One plus One' formula.[44] However, the Conservatives soon had the opportunity to change tactics in the second General Election of December 1910. It is often alleged that nationally this election was simply repetitive, but there had been some shifts in the positions of the main contenders.[45] A crucial additional factor in Norwich was the Conservatives' decision to stand but one candidate, and a 'working man' at that. William Dyson had been a member of Yorkshire Miners' Association between 1877 and 1909 who had sensed the dangers of political trade unionism - 'an evil to be avoided' - and opposed any reversal of the Osborne judgement.[46] In what was clearly an attempt to split the Lib/Lab voting arrangement Dyson offered working class credentials to Labour supporters and non-political trade unionism to the Liberals. His election manifesto stressed, 'For years I have urged upon the Unionist Party the desirability of putting forward workmen candidates . . . to complete their record of work in the interest of the workers, and also of bringing back to their support that large proportion of our electorate who although Unionist in principle have voted since 1900 for trade union and Socialist Labour candidates'.[47] What appeal all this might have had to Norwich workers was undermined by the hideously patronising election slogans adopted, for example 'Will Workman - the Working Mans Candidate', and Dyson's efforts to reassure still less sophisticated Tory voters that he was indeed suitably deferential.

Such Conservative endeavours produced a predictable response from the Liberals and Labour, with both maintaining the electoral arrangement and neither seeking any new ground. Moving the resolution to re-adopt Low as Liberal candidate, A.G. Howlett was obviously intent on spelling out in the simplest possible terms the duty of Liberal voters: 'There were two sections of the Progressive Party. There was another section in addition to the Liberal Party. This other section was loyal to the Liberals last January and the Liberal section were going to be as loyal to them'.[48] Compared with all this, Robert's position was a model of subtlety and sophistication. He described himself as 'a Democrat in politics and a Socialist in economics', stressing that the key issue was the House of Lords and expressing his approval of Free Trade and Home Rule, but going on to record his support for the Minority of the Poor Law Commissioners, for Labour's Right to Work bill and for universal suffrage.[49] Once again the formulation was successful. On a slightly lower turnout Low, with 10,149 votes, was fractionally ahead of Roberts (10,003), while Dyson (7,758) made no impression. Roughly 92% of Low's and Roberts' votes derived from the 'One plus One' arrangement, with little evidence of Tory inroads even on the remaining 8%. Dyson admitted to Tory supporters that 'the splits between Roberts and himself had not reached 300' at his post-election meeting.[50]

The fact that the December 1910 Parliamentary election result approximated closely to that of 1906 is an indication of the Conservative failure to find ways of splitting the joint Labour and Liberal voting pattern in Norwich, though this does not explain why that vote should be so durable. On the latter point, due allowance must be made for the impact of national issues. The Liberal and Labour Parties were on common ground in their commitment to reform of the Lords, to Free Trade and, at least in words, to Home Rule for Ireland, the main features of the election. And, while Roberts could express his desire to increase the pace of social reform, the Liberals could point to their record here by 1910. But can this fully explain why, for example, Labour supporters in General Elections seemed overwhelmingly prepared to vote also for a candidate whose party officials were conniving with the Tories against Labour in municipal matters? Or why so few Liberals were attracted by the lure of an 'anti-Socialist' voting combination of Liberal plus Tory? Either the electorate's grasp of the political situation and of tactical voting was extremely advanced, given the different patterns of municipal voting, or we need to attribute the high 'One plus One' element in the 'Progressive' vote at least partly to the efficient functioning of party machineries and their ability to steer supporters into the desired channels.

If these were features in the Norwich electoral contests in 1910 as in 1906, there was a development in the role which the Labour side had to play. For while there is no direct evidence, ILP membership, municipal voting, local opinion and the Liberals' own behaviour would suggest that Labour was mobilising more of the 'Progressive' vote by 1910, a situation predictable neither in the 1904 by-election nor in 1906, when most commentators accepted that Roberts had relied very heavily upon Liberal voters. Doubtless Labour still needed Liberal votes in 1910 but growing confidence, admittedly at an elated moment, was expressed at Labour's post-election rally. W.R. Smith, the election agent thought they 'had made Mr Roberts' seat secure for all time', while Roberts expressed the view that 'the organisation of the Labour Party was equal to that of the older parties in the city'.[51] And on their part, the Liberals evidently could no longer entertain hopes of fielding two candidates themselves, simply leaving Labour to fend for itself or to inflict what damage it could.

To suggestions that there was common ground on key issues between Liberal and Labour Parties nationally, and that locally Labour had now developed into a major political force, a third factor might be added in explaining the strength of the Lib/Lab arrangement in Norwich. If challenged by the Tories it was not seriously under pressure from mass workplace activity and strikes or the variants of 'Direct Action'. For example, senior Liberal figures such as Howlett and White were not, in their capacity as shoe manufacturers, locked in open conflict with Labour (or Liberal) voting employees.[52] Nor, to continue the example, did prominent ILP figures in the trade union movement find themselves in a position where they would have to compromise or choose sides: what passed for a socialist approach at the Trades Council meeting might have been tested more rigorously on picket lines or in a strike situation.[53] And though one of the best examples of open conflict between Liberals and Labour, the agricultural labourers' dispute at St Faith's, was developing throughout the election campaigning of November and December 1910, the centre of conflict lay outside the Norwich constituency and the open breach was still some weeks away.[54]

Consequently, the strains which trade union struggles might have posed for Lib/Lab electoral arrangements were not likely to be experienced by more than a tiny minority of the Norwich electorate. How else then were voters in the General Elections to gauge the differences in practice between Liberalism and Labourism, particularly if these were being played down by both party organisations? In such a situation it was likely that traditional, radical issues were not disturbed by Labour's rise, and in Norwich the Liberals continued to benefit from these, as did a similarly 'Progressive' Labour Party.[55] The Lib/Lab electoral arrangement worked so well in Norwich because there was relatively little political distance between its adherents in comparison to the one proffered alternative, Toryism.

8

Labour's Electoral Progress
Propulsion and Direction by 1914

The question whether Labour could have held its Parliamentary seat in Norwich independently of the Liberals cannot be definitely answered given their electoral arrangements, but for pointers on this and other issues, evidence from local elections can be utilised. Municipal elections were the focus of sustained activity in which the Labour side found itself ranged against combined Liberal and Conservative opposition, and there was open competition in the Poor Law Guardians' elections. Such conflicts carried class overtones, and information on the social background of Labour and Liberal candidates also throws some light on the class composition and attitudes of their respective parties and upon the longer-term issues of Labour development and Liberal containment.[1]

Given also that Labour had established at least a bridgehead on local government bodies by 1910, its progress over the next few years can be examined not only in numbers of votes amassed, but also in terms of achievement. A feature of socialism in early twentieth-century Britain was its emphasis upon the 'condition of the people' and practical steps to improve this. To a considerable extent this diverted attention away from an examination and remedy of the subordinate class position of workers in capitalist society.[2] Labour Representation had a class element to it, but was presented either as 'socialism' in itself or as a practical step on the road to Socialism, in contrast with utopian dreams or alien and violent revolutionary methods.[3] At the local level it is feasible to ask what were the issues which Labour councillors or Guardians raised, and what difference their presence made, both to the local population and specifically to the Labour Movement. Without expecting small minorities of Labour representatives in Norwich to be capable of transforming the city, it is possible to highlight some of the areas in which Labour councillors and Guardians targeted their efforts.

In a local economy where much of industrial activity was associated with casual or temporary work, and seasonal unemployment or under-employment was high, there was considerable scope for municipal initiative in the area of jobs, working conditions and wages. Correspondingly, this would need to be extensive in order to have more than a minimal impact upon the labour market. Apart from the Poor Law and the occasional Mayoral Fund for relief of the unemployed, the earliest measures to provide work had been via the establishment of a 'Labour Bureau' by local clergy in the 1880s. But since this had been involved in sending unemployed workers from Norwich to help break strikes in Lowestoft in 1886 and in Glasgow in 1891, it was discredited in the local Labour Movement.[4] Subsequently, the practice whereby the Mayor presided over a central fund to provide relief or temporary work was revived in the 1890s, but it was not until the early 1900s that renewed agitation among the unemployed stimulated further change. Both the ILP and some of the more radical elements within the Liberal Party were influential. Roberts, Mayall and Henderson addressed crowds of unemployed workers each December between 1902 and 1905, calling upon the City Council to establish a permanent Labour Bureau to direct public works schemes.[5] Significantly, the self-activity of the unemployed was not referred to by these speakers, or not reported by the local press; either way a contrast to the agitation of the late 1880s.

Though road building and levelling projects were launched by the City Council in 1904 it was not until 1905, and arising from the Unemployed Workmen's Act, that a Distress Committee, comprising fourteen city councillors, ten Guardians and six co-opted members, was formed.[6] This committee at first pursued novel methods, for example financing the emigration of some of the local unemployed to Canada, but such schemes were seen to be totally ineffective when set against the cyclical growth of unemployment by 1908.[7] Public works now became the priority, with 900 temporary jobs provided through the winter of 1908-9, although two-thirds of those employed were dismissed in March 1909 when funds dried up. It was at this point that the ILP claimed that its councillors were decisive in persuading the Norwich MPs to extract additional funds from the Board of Trade, to bring 350 of the local unemployed back on the public works scheme.[8] Even allowing the ILP's full claim, such benefits, while real enough to those directly concerned, amounted only to the temporary extension of temporary work rather than a vindication of practical socialism.

With regard to wages, co-operation between Labour and some Liberal councillors in order to extend the municipal influence over market conditions brought more success. Though the ruling Liberal group's commitment to its Municipal Reform Programme after 1903 was always suspect, Henderson, then a 'Progressive' (Liberal) councillor, promoted the establishment of a Corporation Direct Works department. It paid a minimum of 21 shillings a week to all its employees doing 'normal' work.[9] Further interventions by Henderson and Witard (the ILP city councillor), and by Smith (SDF) and Rev. Cummings (ILP) on the Board of Guardians, in March 1905 extended these arrangements to cover all 400 council workers, who were now to be paid appropriate trade union rates for a forty-eight hour week.[10] This was a boost to both wages and trade unionism in difficult years, yet overall municipalisation had a limited impact in this respect. Only electricity had been municipalised by 1903, and though this generated an annual surplus of some £1,200 by 1909 there was no extension of the programme. Nor were such funds used to reward the workers who had produced them: a suggestion by Councillor Day (ILP) that it was now feasible to reduce the electricity workers' day to eight hours met with no support.[11]

Turning to aspects of social provision, the election of Roberts to the Norwich School Board in 1899 had revealed sharp differences between what the ILP or SDF understood as a social reform package for education and the Liberal and Nonconformist positions. Roberts was unlikely to win much support from other elected members, though he succeeded with two specific measures: the abolition of school fees and the provision of meals for deaf, dumb or blind children in 1900. However, he received no backing for the municipal provision of meals and clothing for other 'necessitous' children.[12] As the School Boards were abolished and their functions placed under Town Council Education Committees under the Education Act of 1902, renewed ILP activity in this area had to wait until Witard was elected as its first councillor in November 1903. Not until September 1905 could he secure council approval for so much as a petition requesting Parliamentary facilities for a School Feeding Bill, as his previous attempts were frustrated by walk-outs by Tory and Liberal councillors alike.[13] With the passing of the Education (Provision of Meals) Act in 1906 the ILP councillors found the going somewhat easier and the Education Committee decided to provide school canteens, additionally levying one eighth of a penny in the pound to finance meals for those children 'unable by reason of lack of food to take full advantage of the education provided for them'.[14] Yet the revelation that more than 600 children were being fed at an annual cost of £1,200 produced an immediate Tory move to reduce this spending, an effort only narrowly beaten off in 1908.[15] Similarly, a battle by Henderson and other ILP councillors in 1908 to persuade the Education Committee to expand its medical services produced only the vague excuse that the council would 'try to provide' medical treatment for those children whose parents were unable to do so.[16]

In other areas of municipal involvement there is little to add in terms of Labour achievement, apart from propagandistic value. In council meetings ILP councillors frequently pressed for the municipalisation of gas, tramways, water supplies and telephones, but more detailed discussions, let alone specific plans, were blocked by Liberals as well as Conservatives. Even municipal housebuilding, first seriously considered when the council had allocated land for its projects in 1899, had failed to develop. What might be achieved by an increased number of Labour councillors remained to be seen. Meanwhile, Conservative majorities swamped Labour endeavours.

This was also essentially the story of the Norwich Board of Guardians. Under the 1894 Local Government Act the franchise for electing Poor Law Guardians had been widened, and in Norwich the size of the Board was expanded to forty-eight members. In the same year Cleverley and Hawkins, standing as 'Trades Council-Trade Union' candidates, had been elected as Guardians, and thereafter a combination of ILP, SDF or Trades Council members made up a minority presence of between two and four. They operated in a narrow and largely hostile environment, for, '... the office of guardian does not seem to have been generally attractive to those seeking civic honours, and was filled largely with small tradesmen, whose first duty was to the rates, members of the clergy and a minority of those genuinely interested in the ... problem of poverty'.[17] Furthermore, in the period under study the Conservatives had held a clear majority until the reforms of 1894 and, though they lost this briefly in the mid-1890s, they had more than recovered so that by 1907 the Board's political composition was thirty-one Conservatives, fourteen Liberals and three Socialist and Trade Unionists.[18]

Unable to exert real influence, the Labour minority's one success came in 1904 when, having proposed that all Poor Law building and repair work be passed automatically to the Corporation's Direct Works Department, W.R. Smith and the Rev. Cummings compromised on an amendment which allowed the Direct Works Department to submit tenders for such work for the first time.[19] This apart, ILP members from 1907 onwards concentrated upon subjecting other Guardians to the public gaze. As the Local Government Board inspector for the Eastern Counties put it, 'Certain socialist members announce and denounce the names of those members who were opposed to the granting of relief'.[20]

To this exercise in public accountability was added a more effective role by 1911, when an ad hoc group of Guardians, including the four Labour members, formed itself into a 'Committee of Investigators' and began to campaign openly for adequate relief rates.[21] Refused access to full documentation by the ruling Tory group, this minority carried out its own investigations, surveying a large sample of those who claimed relief.[22] Its findings included the observations that the average amount of outdoor relief granted to single or aged persons was 4/- per week, for couples without other income, between 7/6d and 8/- per week, for children 2/- per week, while less than 10% of the 900 children surveyed, presumably all 'necessitous', actually did receive a school meal.[23] When the Committee's Report was published in March 1912 it was endorsed by the Trades Council and the ILP and became the subject of public meetings and press correspondence, which ensured that the issues raised figured in the subsequent Guardians' election. Though the Conservatives remained firmly entrenched, growing polarisation was reflected in the rise of the Labour group from five to eight members, and the election of sympathetic independents. The new Board of Guardians comprised twenty-eight Conservatives, ten Liberals, eight Labour and two Independent members.[24] Although the dominant philosophy had not changed, for relief payments did not rise significantly, the Labour group had gathered increased support and was now the effective opposition to the Conservative majority.[25]

This admittedly limited survey of the activities of elected Labour and ILP figures on local government bodies allows a number of conclusions. First, they could have a positive impact alone, or in conjunction with the more 'progressive' of the Liberal councillors, but only when opposition forces were not overwhelming, and only upon very specific issues, such as extending the time scale of public works programmes. More often, Labour initiatives used new legislation as a justification for local measures or as a lever to pull sufficient Liberals, and the odd Tory, to a majority vote, as in the case of school meals arrangements or medical inspection. That such measures were so limited is an indication not only of the small scale of the Labour bridgehead, but also of the absence of any developed social policy or municipal approach amongst most of the Liberal councillors.[26] Perhaps it is significant that in each of the municipal cases examined the 'Radicals', actually Henderson and Day, took the initiative, for example on Corporation rates of pay and conditions of work, or on the 'Direct Works' questions, and that they ended up by joining the ILP. That the much vaunted Liberal Municipal Reform Programme amounted to so little in practice indicates the persistence of an older style Liberalism amongst the businessmen, professionals and shopkeepers who comprised the great bulk of Liberals on municipal and poor law bodies. This has yet to be fully demonstrated, but if it were the case there would be more substance than mere electoral tactics to the 'anti-Labour' alliance which the other two parties seem to have operated after 1907. We would then need to make further allowances for Labour's electoral record and its opportunities to point out real differences between itself and a not-so-radical Liberal Party on aspects of local government.

How is Labour's improving level of representation after 1910 to be explained? To see this in terms of a 'reward' handed by the local electorate to Labour councillors or Guardians for the kind of efforts described above is unconvincing, though Labour's modest attainments still compared well with Liberal or Conservative delivery in these areas. Wider developments, such as more pronounced class-based support for Labour should be included, alongside the possibility that this might be checked by a Liberal revival, notably in the shape of New Liberalism'.[27]

Before concentrating upon these issues, the pattern of local election results can be established. In 1911 Henderson became the second sitting Labour councillor to be re-elected, but at the time this achievement was overshadowed. First, the Liberals made two more gains at the Tories' expense and now looked to be on the way to staging a municipal recovery.[28] Second, Labour was greatly disappointed by its failure to regain lost ground in Catton or to add to its solitary representatives in Mousehold and Wensum wards.[29] In 1912, however, W.R. Smith held his Mousehold seat for Labour

ILP Public Representatives in 1914. Back row from the left: W. Savage (Councillor and Guardian), W. Hindes (Guardian), A. Keeley (Councillor and Guardian), F. Jex (Guardian), E. Manning (Guardian). Front row: W. R. Smith (Councillor and Guardian), Mrs. E. Reeves (Guardian), H. Witard (Councillor).

The Norwich ILP Reception Committee before the National ILP Conference held in the city in 1915.

for a second time, becoming the first Labour candidate to poll over 1,000 votes in a municipal election in the process, while Labour also defeated the sitting Tory in Catton ward, again increasing its vote.[30] Finally, in 1913, H. Witard became the third Labour member to retain a ward in consecutive years, and two further gains were made from the Conservatives. Labour now had two members representing Catton ward, overcoming its disappointment of 1911, and claimed its first success in Heigham ward where, as Bill Holmes explained, 'For a number of years ... the SDF were in the ward, and when they left the ILP was determined that they should assert themselves'.[31] Overall, between 1910 and 1913 the number of Labour councillors had risen from three to six, while the Conservatives had dipped from twenty-eight to twenty-five and the Liberals remained at seventeen.[32]. Electoral evidence thus indicates that the ILP was speaking for more of the Labour Movement in Norwich on the eve of World War One.

How important was social class in Labour representation, and what were its implications for the Labour and Liberal Parties? Aggregate votes cannot be broken down for analysis but it is possible to examine the background of the two parties' local candidates or councillors.[33]

In municipal contests between 1894 and 1913 there were in Norwich forty-six instances of a Labour or socialist candidate standing, and in all but six of these the person concerned was a member of the ILP.[34] Table 2 lists their stated occupations. Involvement as a Labour candidate required not only time and effort, as the question of possible victimisation also had to be considered. This limited the number of potential candidates and indeed caused withdrawals, as seen in the cases of Roberts and Gardiner in 1900.[35] Personal qualities, such as being articulate, confident or even ambitious, might also partly explain why Labour candidates tended to come from 'safer' occupations, areas of white collar or skilled employment, where the risk of victimisation was lessened. Full-time political agents or trade union officials were still less at risk and could be expected to put in the extra time and effort should they be elected. It is likely that H. Cadman, formerly a starch-packer at Colmans, was offered the job of ILP Political Agent for this reason, after being elected in Catton ward in 1907. Apart from the 'gentleman', H.A. Day, and 'others', the only non-working-class occupation was likely to be 'bookseller/newsagent', though this term covered a multitude of activities ranging from shop ownership to shopworker or street news-vendor.[36] Thus the Labour candidates were overwhelmingly working class. Even if they tended to be better off, or 'more respectable' in contemporary parlance, there were still also instances of shoeworker or warehouseman candidates.[37]

How sharp was the contrast with the Liberal Party and its candidates? From the 1880s onwards it was possible to note in Norwich the existence of an 'advanced radical' element which, if not exclusively working class, certainly overlapped with those 'workingmen Liberals' who were active in the local trade unions and could claim some success in the election of Liberal councillors like James Mason, the trade union official, or William Scarlett, a self-employed shoemaker.[38] The social composition of Liberal Radical Clubs in Magdalen Street or Old Palace Road was not likely to be that different from ILP and SDF members or supporters. And 'working-men Liberals' indeed comprised the prime target groups for the ILP and SDF.[39]

Table 2
Occupations of Labour Municipal Candidates[40]

	Labour	Of which ILP
Bookseller/Newsagent	8	7
Political Agent, TU Official	7	5
Insurance Agent	7	7
Shoeworker	6	6
Starch Packer/Warehouseman	3	3
Journalist	3	2
Compositor	2	2
Picture Framer	2	–
Tailor	1	1
Baker	1	1
Boilermaker	1	1
Gentleman	1	1
Other	4	4

Any attempts to organise strictly within the Liberal Party by appealing to what were felt to be the class instincts of its working class supporters were likely to achieve little however. Class struggle or specific working-class interests were not the primary concern, even of 'advanced radical' working-men. Thus when J.J. Colman, Norwich Liberal MP for twenty-four years and 'Mustard Millionaire', died, *Daylight* regretted that he had, '... frequently been held up to opprobrium in the columns of the

Labour Leader, merely because he happened to be a capitalistic employer of a large number of men and boys and girls who did not receive large wages'.[41] But while most working-class Liberals were likely to concentrate on traditional Liberal issues, and though they might attract working class votes in defence of these, just as much as for municipalisation or social reform, they were not in the driving seat of Norwich Liberalism. Ultimately this might be a cause for defections. Aside from the 'Grandees' like J.J. Colman or Sir George White, Norwich Liberalism reflected its middle-class base. The recent study by G.L. Bernstein demonstrates the predominance of business interests and the higher professions among its leading bodies.[42] Thus, of the forty-four Liberals who were elected City councillors at some point between 1899 and 1914, no less than eighteen had business interests as industrialists or merchants, eleven were professionals, including eight lawyers, and twelve were shopkeepers or traders.[43] In addition to the 'gentleman', and subsequent ILP recruit, H.A. Day, this left but two labourers, hardly a sign of a dramatic conversion to broader representation in the higher echelons of the Party, or of inroads made by radical and trade union elements since the mid-1880s.

Though generally denied by the Liberals, here was the basis for class antagonism between Labour and Liberals. While this could be veiled by the tactical considerations of vote-catching or in the interests of great issues such as Free Trade in General Elections, it could not be permanently hidden given the regular contesting of local elections. For one thing, socialists in the ILP such as Bill Holmes constantly emphasised it, and the class base of Liberalism compelled a response. Whatever the limitations of practical socialism the very challenge of Labour represented a threat to Liberal influence, and one which could not for long be brushed aside as some infant idealism. At the local level, as Bernstein puts it, 'socialism was not a theoretical evil which might emerge some day, but an immediate enemy which must be fought and defeated'.[44] Hence the Liberals' reluctance to embark with any real determination upon what was, after all, Henderson's Municipal Reform Programme, and their willingness, once pricked by Labour successes in local government, to work with the Conservatives against Labour and to block what had, before 1906, passed for 'Progressivism' at the local level.

An interpretation which implies that for all its limitations Labour was being propelled by the forces of class identification and consciousness is hardly novel.[45] Neither is it sufficient, for propulsion does not necessarily explain direction, and organised labour in Norwich was still relatively weak. That the ILP, via the Labour Representation Committee, should increasingly be identified with local workers' aspirations suggests some class feeling, but Labour Representation was, at best, a rough pointer, with no indication as to the distance or nature of a Socialist destination. The perseverance of local workers with this form of representation of their interests also requires some explanation. Here the relative weakness of local trade unionism and the absence of alternatives, for example the politics of Direct Action, must figure. It may be that workers in Norwich looked to Labour councillors and the like as an alternative to their own weakness or as a substitute for more direct forms of activity.[46] Perhaps organised labour was also deflected into electoral preoccupation because of economic conditions and the political ideas prevailing locally. When it came to courses of action the exponents of practical socialism in Norwich confined themselves to specific issues, partly because their own political experience and understanding suggested limited electoral advances, partly because the ranged forces of opposition remained strong and intact, and partly because the prospect of active support from the local trade union movement was relatively weak. Yet it could also be suggested that Labour's voice in council chamber or meeting hall did little to realise socialist goals, and that it was not calling upon the general Labour Movement to offer forms of support beyond the act of voting. While the leading Labour figures were mainly working class, it cannot be taken for granted that their occupational background gave them a ready familiarity with a collective workplace approach in their political activities, even had they wished to extend these beyond electoralism.[47]

It would be unreasonable to conclude that those who represented Labour necessarily missed opportunities or consciously held back the local Labour Movement. Yet given the ILP's rise to prominence locally by 1913, its responses to problems and acceptance of limitations would now have greater consequences for the rest of the Movement. If Labour was being propelled by class forces, it was also effectively channelling these.

9

Strategies in the Norwich Labour Movement

c.1880-1914

This study began by contrasting the electoral strength and organisation which the Labour Movement in Norwich developed in this period with its alleged trade union weaknesses. It is doubtful whether the *Labour Leader* of 1894 would have anticipated that Norwich would be among the first cities to return a member of the ILP as a Labour MP in a little over a decade, and that this might happen without any extension of the franchise or decisive improvement in trade union organisation. Simply to outline the course of such developments has been a primary task. But this basic exercise reveals a series of complexities and hints at many more. The fact, for example, that there was a vibrant socialist movement in addition to the longer tradition of radicalism in the city well before the local branch of the ILP was formed was likely to have considerable bearing upon the latter's subsequent growth. Similarly, the development of a 'New Unionism' by no means out of line with the national trends did take place in the late 1880s, only to be checked by a series of counter-measures by employers rather than by its own defects, immaturity or contradictions. Yet just as there were perhaps unexpected strengths in the Labour Movement over the 1880s, so there were areas of weakness not confined to the setbacks suffered by local trade unionism but inherent in the rise of Labour Representation. And certainly trade unionism in Norwich seemed to lack that full complement of ideas and activities seen in some other industrial centres after 1909.

These features cannot be explained solely by reference to those aspects of the local economic and industrial structure which hindered labour organisation, hence a second aim of the study has been to look at the growth of ideas and strategies within the Labour Movement. As we are dealing with a living movement, in which argument and disunity of purpose were ever present, there was inevitably overlap and confusion, but four major themes are discernible for all or most of the period from around 1880 to 1914. There was the effort to 'make socialists', with socialism clearly seen as an alternative, replacement system to capitalism. There was the attempt to permeate the Liberal Party so as to render it more responsive to the needs of the Labour Movement. Later, there was the demand for the separate and distinct political representation of labour interests, and throughout there was trade unionism itself. Along with the impact of contemporary national issues a combination of the above features gave the Norwich Labour Movement its especial characteristics. Was it 'Doing Different', and what light does its experience throw on issues examined by historians?

As trade unionism represents a basic form of workers' organisation which many in the movement would hope to be sufficient to defend or improve conditions of life, it can be seen as a 'strategy' in its own right. It can also be a significant step towards a more advanced class consciousness, when combined with overt political organisation.[1] Sections of this study dealing with trade unionism have noted the existence of all permutations of such combinations between 1880 and 1914, while in the phase associated with 'New Unions', trade unionism itself displayed a considerable degree of initiative and enthusiasm. Around 1888-9 branches of national, new general unions were being formed in Norwich, many of the other local unions took up national issues such as the Eight Hours agitation, and a trade union density of roughly 10% was achieved among male workers.[2] If Norwich trade unionism could not be sustained at these levels over the 1890s and early 1900s there are again national parallels, whether in the decline of general unions, or in the rising level of unemployment and of employers' counter-measures.[3]

Yet there were also specific complications. These included the particular weakness of a competing, Liberal-led local general union, embroiled in those very disputes it sought to avoid, and the migration in of one-time agricultural labourers, which further depressed a labour market already characterised by a high density of temporary or seasonal work and cheap male and female labour.[4] Barring the more skilled crafts, only in the boot and shoe and building industries did local trade unions emerge relatively unscathed from the early 1890s, and then only to suffer a series of setbacks between 1896 and 1900. As a result the nadir of the trade unions, expressed in terms of low membership, an absence of major disputes, and low wages compared with those obtaining in other towns and cities, was reached in Norwich in the early 1900s.

While Norwich had its share of trade union and political activists, their opportunities to intervene in industrial disputes were strictly limited, even between 1909 and 1913. As a result the city was unlikely to become a stronghold of either Direct Action or even strong rank and file movements. What Fred Henderson later described as 'the power generating centre of our strength', the Norwich branches of the National Union of Boot and Shoe Operatives, were sizeable and contained socialist elements, but they were also seen as its weakspots by the national union and were largely quiescent in the years after 1908.[5] The influence of Liberalism and a degree of physical isolation in a large agricultural area also had a retarding effect on trade unionism generally in Norwich. And as this was already in the doldrums in the early 1900s, those ideas and influences which came to the fore elsewhere in shaping the rank and file revolt in 1909-13 did not seem to fit the local Labour Movement's experiences. Thus although there was to be a massive expansion of the unions in the city during wartime conditions, this hardly appeared inevitable in 1914.[6]

A growing emphasis upon electoral politics over the 1890s was by no means unique to Norwich. The apparent failures of the early socialist organisations and the setbacks experienced by trade unions, coupled with the expected opportunities to be derived from exploiting a widening franchise, made forms of Labour Representation an attractive proposition to increasing numbers of workers everywhere.[7] But this path of political and social reform might tend to absorb the efforts of activists at the expense of more traditional aspects of trade union organisation, leaving large numbers of workers to vote for their chosen candidate while being less or not at all involved in workplace trade unionism.[8] Such a scenario cannot solely explain the course of developments in the Norwich Labour Movement, but it may partly account for some of its characteristics. Alleged socialist strength ran concurrent with overall trade union weakness. A good example is the Norwich Amalgamated Society of Railway Servants branch. Here, activists played a key role in the local Labour Representation Committee after 1901, yet they were unable to recruit a sizeable proportion of railway workers, with the consequence that they could not mobilise any real forces for strike action in the national dispute of 1911.[9]

Because there was no mass trade union base in Norwich, the advocates of independent Labour Representation could not guarantee a solid vote either for an ILP candidate in the late 1890s or an LRC one in the early 1900s. A major obstacle was the durability of Liberalism, both within the trade unions and in Norfolk generally. Those within the Labour Movement who sought to permeate the Liberal Party could point out a number of apparent advantages for such a strategy, not least of which was an identification of radical ideas within the Liberal Party, and the formal recognition of a place for skilled labour in the Gladstonian coalition. Again there was nothing peculiar to Norfolk in the fact that democratic reform, free trade, temperance, secular education, religious nonconformity and Home Rule for Ireland were supported. Rather, the significance lay in the extent and sources of that support. Norwich was surrounded by the farmworkers' traditions of Primitive Methodism, and a Liberalism opposed to the Tory trinity of landlord, parson and farmer carried within it overt class connotations. In Norwich itself it was possible to examine a labour-orientated element within Liberalism capable of winning local elections and already, by the late 1880s, prepared to defend its views against 'official' Liberal candidates and to press for the selection of working-men Liberal candidates at Parliamentary level.[10] And over the 1890s and early 1900s some of the 'advanced radicals', often influenced by Fabian thought, were constantly encouraged by people like Fred Henderson to couple their ideas with an openly collectivist approach to social reform and municipal government. This was seen, perhaps most clearly, in the adoption by Norwich Liberals of the Municipal Reform Programme in 1903.

Yet the advantages claimed for such strategies by their proponents within the Labour Movement immediately pale when examined from the perspective of the Liberal Party as a whole. Like the ILP, the Liberals had no ready assembled trade union base among unskilled workers in Norwich, and their involvement through Burgess and Edwards in the Norfolk and Norwich Amalgamated Labour Union was not successful, if the latter body was meant to be a building block for longer-term Liberal electoral purposes. The same could be said in Norfolk generally, where the Liberal-supporting trade unions collapsed amid arable farming recession and wage cutting during the early 1890s. Similarly a replacement body, established in 1906, proved to be more of a trade union than the Liberal 'Grandees' had envisaged, partly because of the socialist element within it. When class struggle surfaced they 'simply could not contain this kind of consciousness and the organisations produced by it'.[11] Local experience of class struggle ran counter to any unifying aspects of New Liberalism nationally and exposed its alleged value to many Norfolk farmworkers.[12]

In Norwich the decline of Liberal influence was both slower and more complex. Class differences, outside and within the Liberal Party, were ever present, and there were clear examples of class struggle between Liberal employers and trade unionists. But their impact was sometimes lessened by early moves towards arbitration, for example in the shoe industry dispute of 1908, or the somewhat more sophisticated policies of divide-and-rule pursued, say, by Colmans when compared to those of Norfolk farmers. Norwich Liberalism was not exposed to those open industrial conflagrations seen in some areas between 1909-13, but a key aspect throughout the years after 1880 was the ability of its leaders to recognise the value of partial concessions. This could be seen in their lip-service to the principle of working-men Parliamentary candidates and acceptance of some municipal ones when under pressure from radicals in the late 1880s.[13]

A more successful policy of containment rested upon encouraging nods in the direction of the national New Liberalism and municipalisation, and harnessing the energies of their advocates within the local Labour Movement. In this light, figures such as Henderson, who became the leading proponent of municipalisation, had a very ambiguous and unwitting role to play. It is not at all clear whether Henderson and 'advanced radicals' within the Party were achieving a breakthrough for the Labour Movement on the municipal front, or on social reform questions, when leading local Liberal figures seemed perfectly happy to use these issues as a means of holding on to working-class support. In practice the Municipal Reform Programme was blocked by Liberal as much as by Conservative councillors, leaving the 'advanced radicals' to defend a less than reformed Liberalism in polemics against the ILP and within the LRC and the trade unions.

Only from around 1906, with the defection of Henderson, Day and others to the ILP, did this Liberal influence begin to break down, though there remained much mileage in 'traditional' Liberal causes. Norwich Liberal leaders relied increasingly upon arrangements with the Tories in municipal contests after 1907, and with Labour in the General Elections of 1906 and 1910, to restrain the advances of what they felt to be the more dangerous enemy in the respective campaigns. This was hardly the action of a party in full control of the local political situation, or of one which felt able to take on all-comers. It marked the onset of that process whereby Liberalism was squeezed between Labour and the Conservatives. More narrowly, the strategy of those workers who sought to utilise the Liberal Party as a vehicle for Labour Representation has to be seen as a failure. Its central aim of electing a working-man Liberal candidate to Parliament was not achieved. All too often this labour-orientated strategy was subjugated to the Liberal leaders and their middle-class supporters.

If the Liberal government on a national scale was under pressure from the Conservative resurgence by 1910, the Norwich Parliamentary election results that year suggest that the Lib/Lab arrangement locally was more than capable of brushing off the Tory challenge. This was testimony to the growing influence by then of separate Labour Representation as a political objective, but also to the closeness, in practice, of Liberal and Labour political positions on matters Parliamentary.[14]

The regrouping of socialists and trade union activists in the early 1890s had contributed to a sizeable, if over-optimistic, beginning for Norwich ILP in 1894. It had struggled to survive, to hold off the challenge of the SDF, and then to preserve its own base against the Liberal-orientated approaches of many radicals in the local Labour Movement. None of these objectives was achieved easily or without incident, but the ILP was developing, through its trade union activity and as prime mover in the city's LRC, into a force which the Liberals could no longer ignore.[15] If dogged by the weakness of local unions, the ILP could take some comfort from the fact that its electoral emphasis was seen as a sound move by many workers. And ironically, the limited leverage that Norwich trade unionism could exert upon the Liberal or Conservative parties was in itself an argument for workers' separate political representation.[16]

At one level the election of G.H. Roberts in 1906 was a resounding success for the strategy of Labour Representation, and especially the ILP. The latter had been the consistent advocate of separate Labour Representation as a principle it had established Roberts as Labour's contender in and after 1904, and had eventually out-flanked other elements within the LRC. Afterwards, Labour had just about held its own in municipal elections during the period of Conservative advance and the Liberal-Conservative agreement after 1907, before coming back strongly to pick up seats against the Conservatives in municipal contests and at the Liberals' expense in Guardians' elections between 1910 and 1913. Into the bargain the ILP had become a mass membership organisation, doubtless with a turnover of members, but clearly the party with which Norwich workers identified. The indications are that in the General Elections of 1910 the Labour influence had grown, and that this was a feature to which the Liberals had to pay far more attention than in 1906. All of this weighs against national interpretations of a Liberal 'containment' of Labour.[17] Nor does the Norwich experience tally with interpretations of a Liberal decline in which the Conservatives rather than Labour were chief beneficiaries.[18]

Such an optimistic view of Labour Representation requires some qualification. Nationally the ILP diluted not only its socialist objectives. It was willing to change the practicalities of Labour Representation by an intended mass Independent Labour Party, socialist in outlook, through accommodations to suit non-socialist trade union leaders, and finally to arrangements with the Liberal Party. All this took less than ten years. In Norwich, Roberts' election successes in 1906 and 1910 were not against the Liberals but still in conjunction with them. Faced by the Conservatives, the two parties needed each other and in practice this meant that the Labour side organised essentially around national issues on which it did not hold the initiative.[19] An alternative, with its starting point in rank and file trade union militancy, was already becoming increasingly popular and exposed Liberalism's antagonisms to the more aroused and confident Labour Movement in the north-west, South Wales, parts of industrial Scotland and the midlands, some of the east coast ports and London. Yet this was not a major feature in Norwich. Consequently the shortcomings of Parliamentary representation, particularly when it involved some form of alliance with the Liberals, from a working class viewpoint were not fully exposed locally. Nor was a critical assessment made of the value of those intensive efforts to elect Labour councillors who, in practice, could do very little to alter the conditions of the great mass of those whom they represented.[20] Here were some less obvious constraints in the Labour Movement, which neither the electors and unenfranchised nor the elected had thoroughly considered.

Additionally, though Labourism went beyond mere electoralism, and while the core of activists grew, there was the point that Labour Representation implied a passivity on the part of the masses of working people other than when casting their votes. And that encouraged a dangerous reliance upon the integrity of those actually elected. On these matters the experience of the Labour Movement in Norwich furnishes further evidence both of the

105

canalising of political support within party channels, for example in the shape of the Lib/Lab voting patterns in Parliamentary elections, and of the less than exemplary behaviour of some figures who were lionised by many of their contemporaries.[21]

Arguably a fourth strategy for the Labour Movement, that of 'making socialists', might have provided safeguards against these flaws in Labour Representation. Certainly the vision of a socialist society as an alternative to the capitalist system was a source of inspiration to early socialists. Had organisations such as the SDF and the Socialist League developed a greater body of theory for their practice and a more precise understanding of the essentials of their objectives, they might have laid the basis for an alternative to the pragmatism of Labour Representation and the more conservative forms of trade unionism. Via the socialist press and the emphasis upon speeches and education, such ideas might travel intact and be applied in allegedly backward or difficult areas like Norfolk.[22]

The experience of the Socialist League between 1885-87 at least would confirm this possibility, for the League made considerable headway and created or attracted a group of socialists, many of whom were key figures in the local Labour Movement long after its own demise. In the short run, at least, it was not the case that the socialism of the Socialist League was 'too strong' or irrelevant to local experiences.[23] In the longer term, failures were predominant. There was the vagueness of the socialist vision, there was the naive assumption that socialists could be made until 'fifty per cent plus one' of the population somehow then achieved the unspecified transformation. And, by no means least, there was the inability to recognise that socialist ideas developed not in a vacuum but out of the struggles of those workers beginning to organise collectively. For all its proportionate strength in Norwich, the League locally was no more on its way to overcoming these problems than elsewhere, and its switch from a policy of 'making socialists' to one of 'making anarchists' was not likely to help matters.

Ironically in the crucial years of 'New Unionism' socialist organisation in Norwich passed its early peak. Revival, in the shape of the SDF, in 1894 resulted in a body more versed in marxist economics but with an even greater emphasis on the educational aspects of making socialists and a still more flawed reliance upon the 'inevitability' of socialism. In Norwich it was a durable competitor with the ILP but one not likely to become a mass organisation and unwilling to relate to those involved in activities outside its familiar domain.

The ILP raised hopes on both these counts, but while pursuing the method of making socialists, actually adapted and distorted this.[24] As described elsewhere, 'emphasis upon making socialists and upon living as socialists provided attractive motifs within ILP propaganda, but were subordinated gradually to the harsh dictates of electoral strategy'.[25] No less than in other cities Norwich ILP had deeply committed members who sought to practise their understanding of a socialist life-style from Labour Church to holiday camp, and who argued the socialist cause in factories, on street corners, upon village greens or at trade union meetings.[26] They gave the ILP its tone, but, for all its opposition to centralist structures, the ILP membership was being led into alliances for Parliamentary objectives. In these socialism, as an alternative to capitalism, had all but ceased to figure. Renewed challenges in the contrasting forms of the British Socialist Party and the workplace-orientated Direct Action were made between 1910 and 1914. Nationally the effect was that the ILP for a time 'appeared irrelevant and tired'.[27] In Norwich, however, neither had any appreciable impact. The strategy of 'making socialists', always a local feature, lacked the orientation upon trade unionism which might have made both that much stronger and instead became subservient to the politics of Labour Representation. Thus the means dominated the end.

The unevenness of the Norwich Labour Movement by 1914 reflected the working out of different strategies in a difficult economic and industrial environment. The influence of the ILP was dominant because the form of Labour Representation it embodied moved along lines of least resistance when compared, say, to open class conflict, and it was the subject of national modification and manipulative alliances. But the failings of earlier generations of socialists, weaknesses of workplace trade unionism, and a local Liberalism which did not contain Labourism, yet sometimes moved tactically under pressure from it, were also important. If assisted by rising class feelings, Norwich ILP had no ready-made trade union building blocks to hand.[28] Its own membership, of around 500 between 1905 and 1908, became the central force in the local Labour Movement, and the basis of Labour's electoral strength. That was a genuine achievement, yet even this membership was part of that audience in the name of which something, one cannot really say socialism, might be provided by elected councillors and MPs. Such rewards were satisfying to most in the Labour Movement, acceptable to the bulk of the Liberals, and tolerable even for many Conservatives by 1914. Whether the direction of the Norwich Labour Movement's development was still that pointed out by the Socialists of the mid-1880s, and whether the scenario was that envisaged by the first 'New Unionists', was altogether more questionable.

Notes

Chapter 1

1. Cited in *Daylight*, 23 June 1984.
2. E.P. Thompson, *William Morris: Romantic to Revolutionary* (2nd ed., New York 1976), (hereafter Thompson, *William Morris*), pp.460-1.
3. See *Board of Trade, Statistical Tables and Report on Trade Unions*, 10, (1897) (hereafter BoT *Reports*); H.A. Clegg, A. Fox and A.F. Thompson, *A History of British Trade Unions since 1889*, 1 (Oxford 1964) (hereafter *British Trade Unions*) pp.179-181.
4. eg. A. Fox, *A History of the NUBSO 1874-1957*, (Oxford 1958) (hereafter Fox, *History of NUBSO*); R. Groves, *Sharpen the Sickle!* (London 1949) (hereafter Groves, *Sickle*); W.L. Sparks, *The Story of Shoemaking in Norwich* (Norwich 1949) (hereafter Sparks, *Shoemaking*); F. Bealey and H. Pelling, *Labour and Politics 1900-1906* (London 1958) (hereafter Bealey and Pelling, *Labour and Politics*) provide some information on the Norwich Labour Movement at election times.
5. See C.B. Hawkins, *Norwich, A Social Study* (London 1910) (hereafter Hawkins, *Norwich*); A. Howkins, *Poor Labouring Men: Rural Radicalism in Norfolk 1870-1923* (London 1985) (hereafter Howkins, *Labouring Men*); and G.L. Bernstein 'Liberalism and the Progressive Alliance in the Constituencies 1900-14' *Historical Journal*, 26, (1983) (hereafter Bernstein, 'Liberalism') 617-640. I am grateful to Fred Whitmore for the opportunity to examine his 'The Labour Party, Municipal Politics and Municipal Elections in Norwich 1903-33' prior to its publication. These help to remedy a small deficiency in D. Howell's monumental *British Workers and the Independent Labour Party 1888-1906* (Manchester 1983) (hereafter Howell, *British Workers*) which does not consider Norwich as one of its models of ILP development.
6. *The Eastern Daily Press* (hereafter *EDP*) was the main Liberal newspaper. Respectively these others were *Sword and Shield* (1890), *Eastern Star* (1891-2), and *Eastern Weekly Leader* (hereafter *EWL* (1894-6). These covered the growth of New Unionism and the General Elections of 1892 and 1895. *Citizenship* (1902) was the product of Fred Henderson, then permeating the Liberal Party, while the *Norwich Elector*, later *Norwich Labour Elector* (1904-06) was established by Norwich ILP.
7. Norwich Central Library (hereafter NCL), Local Studies Department has boxes of local election broadsheets, newspaper cuttings etc. catalogued under the heading *Norwich Municipal Corporation Addresses etc.* (hereafter *NMCA*).
8. By 'active to passive' is meant the switch in emphasis from regular self activity, often with revolutionary implications, to the occasional and more mechanistic spates of local electioneering by socialist individuals and organisations. Very much related to this was the rise of 'New Liberalism' and, more importantly, changes in the role and scope for socialists in the workplace.
9. cf. H. Pelling, *The Origins of the Labour Party* (Oxford 1965) (hereafter Pelling, *Origins of Labour Party*); and P.F. Clarke, *Lancashire and the New Liberalism*, 1971 (Cambridge 1971) (hereafter Clarke, *Lancashire*); and K. Laybourn, *The Rise of Labour* (London 1988).
10. All figures in this paragraph are derived from the *Census Reports* of 1881, 1891, 1901 and 1911.
11. Hawkins *Norwich*, p.65.
12. These figures refer to the percentages of occupied males aged over 10 years and not retired. It is likely that all are underestimates, as casual work, a feature of these industries, was much less well recorded.
13. *Jarrolds Norwich Directory*, Norwich, 1896. See also Fox, *History of NUBSO*, and M.G. Adams, 'The Norwich Boot and Shoe Trade 1870-1914' (unpublished MA Dissertation University East Anglia, 1971) (hereafter Adams, 'Norwich Boot and Shoe Trade').
14. The low age limit of 10 years is used here because this is common to all census returns in the period under study, while the 40-45% estimate tries to allow for the majority of girls aged between 10 and 15 years who were not working. In all the 1891, 1901 and 1911 data I have calculated the 'Occupied Population' as the data given for the population aged 10 years or more, minus the 10-14 age group, minus those aged over 65 years. plus the 10-14 year olds known to have been working. This gives a figure for the 15-65 age group working, plus the working 10-14 year olds, though it does not allow for those working beyond the age of 65.
15. An average of 650 women did charring work with a further 800 in laundry, washing etc. between 1881-1911. Office cleaning at rates of 3/6d to 5/- a week was the most regular work, according to Hawkins, *Norwich* , p.59.
16. *ibid*, p.60. Calculations from the 1901 Census indicate that 21% of boys and 17% of girls aged between

10 and 14 years were working.

17. As will be seen the Norwich shoeworkers did not play such a role, despite their apparent potential.

18. Board of Trade, *Report on Strikes and Lockouts in the UK* 1 (1888) (hereafter BoT, *Strikes*), 21-9.

19. *EWL*, 31 August 1895.

20. G. Thorn, 'The Early History of the Amalgamated Society of Boot and Shoemakers', *Bulletin of the Society for the Study of Labour History*, 39, (1979), p.23.

21. ASE figure in BoT, *Reports*, 5, (1891); ASCJ figure cited in F. Chandler, *History of the Amalgamated Society of Carpenters and Joiners*, (Manchester 1910), p.43. A second branch with forty-nine members was formed in 1883 according to *EWL*, 19 November 1894.

22. See Groves, *Sickle*, p.64 and BoT, *Reports*, 4, (1889-90).

23. W. Holt 'Norwich Co-operative Society', *Souvenir of the 69th Trade Union Congress*, edited by E. Pointer (hereafter Pointer, *69th TUC*) (Norwich 1937), p.105.

24. *Daylight*, 23 May 1885.

25. See Howkins, *Labouring Men*, Chapter 3 for more detailed discussion.

26. Groves, *Sickle*, p.88.

27. Nonetheless the 'coalition of interests', (Home Rule and Temperance could be added to the features already mentioned) had a good deal of mileage left in it. The renewed value of Free Trade, and 'New Liberalism', as issues which focused attention away from class conflict was still to be seen.

28. *Daylight*, 30 May 1885.

29. *ibid*, 3 October 1885.

30. *ibid*, 7 November and 19 December 1885. Meetings were now held at the Gordon Cafe, run by Slaughter.

31. Bullard polled 7,279 votes compared with Colman's 6,666. The second Liberal, Wright, failed to secure election with 6,251 votes. *Daylight*, 27 March and 10 April 1886.

32. *ibid*, 10 April 1886.

33. NCL, Local Studies Dept., *NMCA*, November 1886.

34. J. Mason was a union official in NUBSO, elected as a Liberal in Catton ward in 1890. Williment was Secretary to the Norwich Friendly Societies' Medical Institute. He was elected in Heigham ward in 1892.Scarlett was a small scale shoemaker, rather than a shoeworker, elected in Wensum ward in 1893. All were local Liberals and were regularly re-elected in these mainly working class wards east and north of the city.

Chapter 2

1. A full branch of the SDF was not formed in Norwich until 1894. For a general account see C. Tsusuki, *H.M. Hyndman and British Socialism* (London 1961) (hereafter, Tsusuki, *Hyndman*.

2. Sympathisers might point to the overreliance upon education rather than collective struggles of workers. Opponents suggest that revolutionary socialist ideas are of no interest to British workers, not practicable, or simply utopian.

3. *Daylight*, 13 February 1886, and *Commonweal*, 2, 14 (March 1886).

4. Norfolk Record Office (hereafter NRO) J.F. Henderson, Correspondence, HEN 1. A document in this collection names eleven members at an early meeting: of these F. Slaughter, T. Morely, A. Moore, A. Darley, A. Houghton, H. Parker, S. Mills, G.F. Hipperson, S. Gostling were committee members of the enlarged branch in 1886 and 1887.

5. *Commonweal*, 2.15 (April 1886).

6. This speech was reproduced in full as a Supplementary Issue of *Daylight*, 13 March 1886, a measure of the local interest being shown, not least by Burgess.

7. J. McFarlan, 'Fred Henderson of Norwich', Radio broadcast script, 24 June 1952, p.10, NCL. Mowbray was brought to Norwich by Slaughter. Henderson was born in Norwich and initially attracted to revolutionary socialism via the poetry of Shelley and meetings with Morris.

8. *Commonweal*, 2.27 (July 1886), 2.16 (17 May 1886). The paper was now fortnightly.

9. *ibid*, 2.41 (23 October 1886).

10. *Daylight*, 13 November 1886; *Commonweal*,.2.46, (27 November) and 2.49, (18 December 1886).

11. *Commonweal*, 2.15 (April 1886).

12. Pelling, *Origins of Labour Party*, p.215.

13. *Commonweal*, 2.16 (May 1886).

14. *ibid*, 2.41 (23 October 1886).

15. *ibid*, 2.42 (30 October 1886) and 2.48 (11 December 1886).

16. *ibid*, 2.15 (April 1886). Morris compared Norwich favourably with Liverpool, where the socialists he had lectured to were more cautious and considerate of trade unionism and electioneering.

17. *ibid*, 2.41, (23 October 1886).

18. *ibid*, various issues in 1886. In the case of St Faiths, for example, an anonymous SL member described how 'on Friday nights our members have tramped the six miles along a bad road in all kinds of

weather, always sure of finding the room filed with men anxious to hear the new gospel.' Cited in Thompson, *William Morris*, p.418.

19. *Daylight*, 15 January 1887.
20. *ibid*, 11 December 1886.
21. *ibid*, 8 January 1887. Haldensteins paid the lowest rates among the main shoe manufacturers locally and had defeated a strike in February 1883. They also practised 'Grindery', the deduction from wages of charges for heating, lighting and even 'work space' for those working on site.
22. 'Statement by the Temporary Committee for the Relief of the Unemployed', as reported in *Daylight*, 27 February 1886.
23. So called because the first policeman on the scene, deciding to concentrate upon his notebook, informed the court at the trial of Henderson and Mowbray, 'I saw a ham run over the heads of the crowd' (*Daylight*, 22 January 1887).
24. As Mowbray was being struck with this at the time, he had grabbed and hurled it up the street. Police searches of the crowd revealed the following weaponry: two small stones, two feet of broomstick, one cabbage stalk and a bottle containing what proved to be ginger beer (*ibid*, 22 January 1887).
25. *ibid*, 21 May 1887.
26. Thompson, *William Morris*, p.461. The Conference was held on 29 May 1887.
27. Principal speakers were Mowbray, Morely, Adams, Parker, Reynolds, Poynts, Darley and Henderson.
28. *Daylight*, 7 May 1887.
29. Thompson, *William Morris*, p.463, p.517 refers to letters concerning 'a crisis in the Norwich branch' and identifying Henderson as an 'anarchist leader'.
30. *Daylight*, 9 July 1887. Sexual questions, involving 'Free Love' and criticism of the Family were all too much for Burgess, who had previously given the League what he considered to be a favourable press.
31. *ibid*, 27 July 1887.
32. Moving to London, he worked as a reporter on 'The Star', but also briefly edited 'The Leader and Workers Advocate' (Sept/Oct 1891). More influenced by George Bernard Shaw now than Morris, he had published a volume of poems in 1892 and even considered becoming a professional actor. He maintained his links with Norwich (he had married Lucy Slaughter, a sister of Fred Charles) but his contributions on his return to the city were stamped by Progressivism, 'independence' — even self-interest — rather than revolutionary socialism.
33. *Daylight*, 18 August 1888.
34. See J. Quail, *The Slow Burning Fuse - the lost history of Britain's Anarchists* (London 1978), p.69.
35. Thompson, *William Morris*, p.506; *Daylight*, 8 December 1888.
36. This will be discussed below. The anarchists' meetings were sustained in Norwich and occasionally in St Faith's from 1888 to 1892. See *Eastern Star*, 22 August 1891, and *Daylight*, 3 October 1891.
37. See, for example, A.L. Morton and G. Tate, *The British Labour Movement*, (London 1956) pp.176-184, or M. Haynes, 'The British Working Class in Revolt 1910-14'; *International Socialism*, 2nd Series 22 (1984) 101-7.
38. Cited in R. Groves, *Sickle*, p.101.
39. Crotch was very close to the SL and may briefly have been a member, see *Daylight*, 21 May 1887.
40. Cited in Groves, *Sickle*, p.104.
41. In this case the Socialist League had issued leaflets to the workers and held a meeting and fundraising concert on their behalf. *Daylight*, 10 and 24 March 1888.

Chapter 3

1. *Daylight*, 24 October 1885. The delegate, W.T. Scarles, probably represented the Amalgamated Society of Plasterers.
2. The Committee included Scarles, Vines (a socialist shoeworker) and Hawkins, the former Chartist who became the Trades Council's first Secretary when it was formally established in 1886. (*Daylight*, 31 October 1885).
3. *ibid*, 21 November 1885.
4. *Daylight*, 14 August 1886 and 22 January 1887.
5. H. Palmer 'Trade Unionism in Norwich' in Pointer 69th TUC p.99, R. Groves, *Sickle*, pp.85-6.
6. When the Clickers' Union merged into the NUBSO in 1892 many Norwich shoeworker members remained outside, reverting to the old independent body. This then lost members to NUBSO and collapsed by 1894, at which point a Clickers NUBSO branch (Norwich No.2) was formed.
7. *Rules and Orders of the NNALU* (Norwich 1895) Rule 7.
8. *Sword and Shield*, 21 June 1890.
9. *Daylight*, 30 August 1890.
10. *ibid*, 8 November 1890.
11. *ibid*, 17 January 1891. The Norwich District of the new union contained eleven branches. George

Edwards became its Treasurer and Organiser.
12. *Sword and Shield*, 7 and 15 June 1890.
13. *Daylight*, 9 August 1890.
14. *ibid*, 25 October 1890. Only 43 union members were re-employed.
15. *ibid*, 3rd January 1891.
16. Prominent in the demands for Labour Representation in 1890 was Bill Holmes, soon to be a founder member of Norwich ILP. Burgess described these events only years later in *Daylight*, 29th February 1908.
17. Miller, Chairman of the NNALU, reported in *Eastern Star*, 6 June 1891.
18. F. Howes, Executive Committee member, *ibid*.
19. The ASHD was founded in February 1890, with thirty members. The TA, founded in May, still had less than twenty-five members a year later (*Eastern Star*, 9 May 1891).
20. *Sword and Shield*, 31 May 1890.
21. *ibid*, 14 June 1890. Interestingly, it was reported that 'For a long while the Executive at Union HQ have felt that something must be done to place Norwich workmen on an equal footing (!) with other towns' (*Daylight*, 14 June 1890).
22. *Daylight*, 14 June 1890. The strike figures cited were likely to be an overestimate, as many of the 'strikers' were actually locked out. BoT, *Strikes* 3, (1890) 63.
23. *Sword and Shield*, 5 July 1890.
24. *Daylight*, 2 August 1890.
25. The strike ran from 6 December 1890 to 7 February 1891. *ibid* and 20 December 1890, 7 February 1891.
26. *ibid*, 24 January, 7 February, 28 February and 7 March 1891.
27. *Eastern Star*, 3 October 1891.
28. *ibid*, 23 May 1891; *Daylight*, 30 May 1891.
29. *Eastern Star*, 6 June 1891.
30. The 'extra' ½d was not paid, for BoT *Reports* 5 (1891) and 6 (1892), show standard rates in Norwich at 6½d and not 7d per hour.
31. *Eastern Star*, 10 October 1891.
32. Out of twenty local branches of skilled unions the known memberships were: OBS 257, ASE 106, ASCJ 200+, Brushmakers 100, Steam Engine Makers 67, Painters and Decorators 50, Plumbers 29, Boiler Makers 24, TA 25. Even if the other skilled societies such as the Stonemasons, Bakers or Ironfounders had tiny memberships the overall estimate of 900 is a conservative figure.
33. *EWL*, 16 March 1895.
34. *Daylight*, 17 January 1891.
35. As a rough cross check, 3,000 trade unionists were affiliated to the Norwich Trades Council according to its Fourth Annual Report, cited in *Daylight*, 17 January 1891.
36. *ibid*, 9 May 1891. The lower estimate cited in *Eastern Star*, 9 May 1891.
37. *Daylight*, 19 September 1891.
38. *ibid*, 22 August 1891.
39. *ibid*, 22 August and 26 September 1891.
40. *Eastern Star*, 6 June 1891 and BoT, *Reports*, 5 (1891). Membership fell further, to 675 at the end of 1893 and to 400 in December 1894.BoT, *Reports*, 10 (1897) 77.
41. *Daylight*, 28 May 1892. BoT, *Reports*, 6, (1892).
42. *Daylight*, 2 April 1892.
43. *ibid*, 28 May 1892.
44. *ibid*, 8 July 1893.
45. *ibid*, 13 January 1894.
46. *ibid*, 25 March 1893 and 17 February 1894. TA Branch membership had just topped 100 while the Machine Rulers' branch was reported to cover one third of those working in this area.
47. *ibid*, 8 April 1894. The ASRS did expand, by '30 or 40' according to the *EWL*, 3 November 1894, but this growth was not maintained.
48. Between 1896 and 1900 the numbers recovered slightly, averaging 2,600. The number of trade union branches affiliating to the Trades Council fell, however, from 22 in 1894 to 18 in 1898. BoT, *Reports*, 10 (1897), 204-5 and 14 (1901), 150.
49. *Daylight*, 25 March 1893.
50. *ibid*, 8 September 1894.
51. *ibid*.
52. *ibid*.
53. 'Report of the Congress Committee' in Norwich Trades Council, *Eighth Annual Report* (Norwich 1894), p.9. The delegates spent a good deal of time outside the city, travelling by special train to Cromer for a Garden Party, courtesy of Sir Samuel Hoare MP, and then by carriages to Carrow, for a Garden Party at the expense of J.J. Colman MP.
54. Respectively in BoT *Strikes*, 9 (1896), item 651 and 11 (1898), item 287; *Daylight*, 26 August 1899.

55. *Daylight*, 9 September 1899.
56. See Fox, *History of NUBSO*, 1958, p.227, and Clegg, Fox and Thompson, *British Trade Unions*, p.165.
57. BoT, *Labour Gazette*, February 1894, p.4, *Daylight*, 2 June and 14 July 1894.
58. *EWL*, 11 May 1895.
59. BoT, *Strikes*, 9, (1896) 8-9.
60. *ibid*, 12 (1899) 78-9.
61. *ibid*, 14, (1901) 2-3; and Norwich Trades Council, Executive Committee Minutes, 4 June 1901.
62. BoT, *Strikes* 13, (1900) 8-9; *Daylight*, 11 August 1900; *Norfolk Socialist Review*, 3 and 5 (1901).
63. *EWL*, 9 November and 7 December 1895. The 1896 strikes were smaller, respectively involving 82, 31 and 40 workers. BoT *Strikes* 9, (1896) 112-3.
64. *EWL*, 19 October 1895. Votier also suggested that women's wages were a drag on overall wages. The solution he proposed was neither the better organisation of working women, nor equal pay, but factory production which, presumably by making more of the women redundant, 'would improve the home life'.
65. *Daylight*, 20 February 1897.
66. BoT *Strikes* 10 (1897) 145; *Daylight*, 27 February and 4 March (1897).
67. *Daylight*, 22 May and 19 June 1897. Between 2 and 3,000 attended the demonstration.
68. *Norfolk News*, 23 October 1897.
69. *ibid*.
70. It emerged subsequently that at one point in the strike Mason, besieged by strikers and with no money from the union's Head Office, had gone to fellow Liberal Sir George White MP, leader of the employers' side, to request a loan. This then financed the strikers in need for that week (W. Sparks, *Shoemaking* (Norwich 1949), p.50).
71. Fox *History of NUBSO*, cites a membership figure of 345 in 1905 (p.316). The estimate of 400 in 1900 is in Adams, 'The Norwich Boot and Shoe Trade', p.77.
72. *Daylight*, 28 May 1892.

Chapter 4

1. See for example M. Beer, *A History of British Socialism*, (London 1919), II chapter 15 and Pelling, *Origins of Labour Party*, chapter 3 for outlines of these developments.
2. See for example, Howell, *British Workers*, p.285.
3. Though F. Crotch was elected as an 'independent socialist' councillor in 1886 he was incorporated into the Liberal Group and remained a rather minor figure within it, as did the other workingmen Liberals elected.
4. *Daylight*, 2 June 1888. The paper ran a series of editorials slanted at workers and 'advanced' radicals on the 'Where are your Liberal leaders?' theme (*ibid*, 8 October, 19 November 1887).
5. *ibid*, 11 July 1891.
6. *ibid*, 27 February 1892. Tillett's letter to Burgess was dated 18 July 1891, though its contents were not published for six months.
7. *ibid*, 5 September 1891.
8. *ibid*, 12 September 1891.
9. *Eastern Star*, 5 September 1891.
10. The first of what became a series of such 'debates' was held on 11 October, at which Mowbray addressed a crowd of 'several thousands' (*Daylight*, 3 and 17 October 1891).
11. *Eastern Star*, 17 October 1891. Letter from J. Bedford.
12. *Daylight*, 24 and 31 October 1891.
13. *ibid*, 5 December 1891.
14. Respectively reported in *Daylight*, 17 February, 11 June and 4 July 1892.
15. Sir Samuel Hoare (Con) 7,718 votes and J.J. Colman (Lib) 7.407 votes, were both elected. Bedford (Lib) with 6,811 votes was in third place.
16. The new Radical Club was in Botolph Street (*Daylight*, 16 July 1892).
17. *ibid*, 16 July 1892, letter from F.H. Green.
18. *ibid*, 21 January 1893.
19. See Pelling, *Origins of Labour Party*, p.192.
20. *Daylight*, 15 September 1894. For other ex-SL members see Ch.2 above.
21. NCL, Local Studies Dept., *NMCA*, 1894; *Daylight*, 13 and 27 October 1894.
22. About 10 members formed the Norwich SDF branch in March 1894, including W.R. Smith, soon to be a major figure in the local Labour Movement, and the four Segon brothers. *Norwich Labour Elector*, 20, 21, 22, September-November 1906.
23. NCL, Local Studies Dept., *NMCA* 1 November 1894. The SDF emphasised particularly the need for a municipal housebuilding programme.
24. *Daylight*, 1 June 1895.

25. *ibid*, 13 July 1895, and *EWL*, 18 January 1896.
26. *Daylight*, 7 May and 6 July 1895.
27. Quelch, the Editor of the SDF paper, *Justice*, was in Norwich during this campaign. *Daylight, Election Special*, 9 July 1895.
28. *EWL*, 24 August 1895.
29. *Daylight, Election Special*, 16 July 1895.
30. In Norwich the Tories, Sir Samuel Hoare and Sir Harry Bullard, were elected with more than 8,000 votes each. The Liberal candidates, Terrell and Verney, polled 7,329 and 7,210 votes respectively.
31. *EWL*, 17 August 1895.
32. *ibid*, 28 August 1895.
33. *ibid*, 5 October 1895. The SDF castigated Barnes and other ILP members 'who tried to build up a movement in ignorance of economics ... (they) ... were building castles in the air and would as assuredly fail in their efforts as the Chartists and Owenite Socialists failed years ago'.
34. *Daylight*, 11 January 1896. Bill Moore, then ILP Secretary, claimed the active membership had fallen to just seven at one point in 1895.
35. *ibid*, 1 February 1896.
36. *ibid*, 5 September 1896.
37. *ibid*, 28 March 1896.
38. *ibid*, 28 November 1896. Sutton received 6,913 votes, compared with the 13,200 for Burgess, who topped the poll.
39. NCL, Local Studies Dept., *NMCA*, Election Poster, 1897. Sixteen seats fell vacant and each party had eight sitting members.
40. *Daylight*, 16 October 1897. Evidently ILP members tried the same tactic.
41. *ibid*, 24 July and 4 September 1897.
42. *ibid*, 17 July 1897. The gain was temporary, as Cleverley was returned again in 1898, while Mason, the NUBSO Branch Secretary and Liberal councillor, retained his post as Trades Council President in 1897.
43. *ibid*, 29 January 1898. On the fusion issue, see Pelling *Origins of Labour Party*, p.219-220 and Howell *British Workers*, pp.10-12.
44. In 1899 G.H. Roberts became President of the Norwich branch, having joined in 1896. Holmes had now established a considerable base in the GGLU, and Witard, soon to be the ILP's first Councillor, had returned to Norwich.
45. *Daylight*, 30 September 1899.
46. *Justice*, 2 December 1899, cited in B. Simon, *Education and the Labour Movement 1870-1920* (London 1965), p.152.
47. *Daylight*, 25 November 1899.
48. *ibid*, 12 May 1899.
49. *ibid*, 23 June 1900.
50. *ibid*, 4 May 1901.
51. See 'The ILP in Norwich', *ILP 23rd Annual Conference Souvenir* (Norwich 1915); *Norfolk Socialist Review*, No.3 March 1901.
52. These aspects are the subject of Chapter Six, below.
53. Considering the extent and qualifications of the franchise, probably 40% of all adult males, including a higher proportion of working class men, as well as all women, were denied the vote in Parliamentary elections at this time.

Chapter 5

1. See, for example, Clegg, Fox and Thompson, *British Trade Unionism*, pp.326-340, BoT, *Abstract of Labour Statistics* (hereafter BoT *Abstracts*) 17 (1913/14).
2. See, for example, M. Haynes, 'Strikes', in *The Working Class in England 1875-1914*, edited by J. Benson (London 1985), particularly pp.92-5. The BoT, *Labour Gazette*, October 1911, p.390, recorded a strike by 196 clickers and finishers in mid September.
3. BoT, *Reports* 9 (1901), 150; 12 (1906-7), 129 and 14, (1910-11), 125.
4. *ibid*
5. *ibid* 10 (1902-4) and 17 (1914).
6. NCL, Local Studies Dept., *Norwich Trades Council Executive Committee Minute Book* (hereafter TCEC), 4 June 1901. The remaining trade union was the Gasworkers and General which lost members, but survived.. See *Norwich Elector*, No.7, August 1905.
7. NCL, Local Studies Dept., TCEC 16 December 1901 and 23 January 1902. See *Daylight*, 12 May 1900 for an account of working conditions here.
8. The Society had only 'about 50' members in 1910 (Hawkins, *Norwich*, p.50).
9. *Norfolk Socialist Review*, 1 (1901), p.11.

114

10. *Norwich Elector*, 7 (July 1905).
11. *ibid*, 8 (September 1905).
12. *Daylight*, 29 March 1902; BoT, *Abstracts*, Vol.13, 1907-8 44.
13. *Daylight*, 5 July 1902; Hawkins, *Norwich*, p.55.
14. *Norwich Elector*, 2 (March 1905) claimed that there had been 500 GGLU members at Colmans in the early 1900s, though this seems a high figure and may refer to the total GGLU membership in Norwich. Certainly it was said that there were only 'a few handsful' of members at Colmans when Holmes became Secretary in 1908. Total GGLU membership in Norwich was 1,100 in 1914, according to H. Palmer, 'Trade Unionism in Norwich', in E. Pointer, *69th TUC*, p.100.
15. *Norwich Elector*, No.4, (May 1905).
16. Hipperson was also ILP Branch Secretary and Holmes was on the TCEC. Other ILP members holding union positions were E. Manning (Typographical Association), F. Easton (Secretary, Newsagent and Booksellers), C. Jermy (Amalgamated Society of Bakers and Confectioners), H.J,. Cadman (GGLU) and C. Savage, H. Fraser and F. Jex (all members of NUBSO) All bar the last two stood as ILP candidates in municipal elections before 1913.
17. NCL, Local Studies Dept., TCEC, 7 March 1905. The May Day demonstration may well have reflected the ILP bases as the 'good contingents' were from the Bricklayers', Plasterers', GGLU, Bakers' and NUBSO. *Norwich Elector*, 4 (May 1905).
18. NCL, Local Studies Dept., TCEC, 4 January 1906.
19. *ibid*, passim 1904-1908
20. *ibid*, 29 April 1907.
21. *ibid*, 7 September 1908. 27 women struck at the end of August.
22. The 'National Picture' here is interpreted as a rise in the number of strikes from 1909 to a peak in 1913, an increase in the number of strikers from 1909 to a peak in 1912, and a rise in the number of days taken in strikes from 1909 to a peak in 1912.
23. See for example, J. Hinton, 'The Rise of a mass Labour Movement: Growth and Limitations' and J.E. Cronin, 'Strikes 1870-1914', in *A History of British Industrial Relations 1875-1914*, edited by C. Wrigley (Brighton 1982), (hereafter Wrigley, *British Industrial Relations*) pp.20-46 and pp.47-73.
24. Adams, 'Norwich Boot and Shoe Trade', p.62.
25. *Norwich Elector*, 13 (February 1906).
26. There were 1980 union members, including 160 women by the end of 1907 (Adams, *Norwich Boot and Shoe Trade*, p.80). Fox, *History of NUBSO* p.316, refers to a probationary membership of over 1,700 new or recent recruits out of a peak total of 3,148 members at the close of 1908.
27. *Daylight*, 11 and 18 January 1908.
28. *ibid*, 29 February 1908.
29. BoT, *Labour Gazette*, February 1914, p.69. The pay claim of 1913 was not resolved until 5 January 1914, when 1,000 workers obtained a further 1/- on minimum wages.
30. Fox, *History of NUBSO*, p.317.
31. See Howkins, *Labouring Men*, and Groves, *Sickle*. To these sources I owe a particular debt for the brief account given here.
32. Two of the union's Executive Committee were Liberal M.P.s and the farmworker members were all Liberals. Groves, *Sickle*, p.106.
33. Howkins, *Labouring Men*, p.96; Groves *Sickle*, p.115. Founder members of the EASU here included Branch Secretary George Hewitt, who had been in the Socialist League and was now a member of the ILP and W. Norgate, another socialist.
34. Groves, *Sickle*, pp.118, 121.
35. Howkins, *Labouring Men*, pp.106-8. 'Clarion' supporters and ILP members had revived socialist propaganda trips in rural areas in 1903, but these were stepped up in 1906-7 and particularly in 1908, when Holmes became ILP Eastern Counties Organiser.
36. Groves, *Sickle*, pp.119, 124. The amount raised by these collections varied from £12-£20 - sufficient to provide an extra 1/- to 3/- for those on strike pay.
37. Walter Smith became the new President and Holmes was also elected to the new Executive. The union became the National Agricultural Labourers and Rural Workers Union in 1912.
38. Howkins, *Labouring Men*, pp.106-8.
39. Clegg, Fox and Thompson, *British Trade Unionism*, 1 (1964), 230-1. The ASRS strongholds were remote from both the Great Eastern Railway and the Midland and Great Northern Joint Railway in terms of geography and rail links.
40. The Norwich ASRS branch supported G.H. Roberts as ILP candidate against the Liberal L. Tillett in the Parliamentary by-election of 1904. See R. Bagwell, *The Railwaymen* (London 1963), pp.234-5.
41. *EDP*, 4, 6, 14 and 15 August 1911.
42. *ibid*, 18 August 1911. The press report was headed 'Quietude at Norwich Thorpe'. Elsewhere there was 'very little appearance of a strike at Kings Lynn', 'No strike scenes in Yarmouth' and 'little anxiety' at Ipswich.

115

43. *EDP*, 22 August 1911 Circular from GER General Manager W.H. Hyde.
44. *EDP*, 18 August 1911 J.J. Petine, interviewed.
45. *EDP* 19 August 1911.
46. Apart from two members on the Strike Committee no employee of the GER was present (*EDP*, 19 August 1911).
47. *EDP*, 19 August 1911.
48. Clegg, Fox and Thompson *British Trade Unionism*, p.351. Trade Union density declined from 19% in 1901 to 13% in 1910 (p.468).
49. BoT, *Abstracts* 10, (1902-04), 17, (1914). Carpenters and Joiners, Bricklayers and Plumbers achieved an 8½d/hr rate in June 1914. BoT *Labour Gazette*, July 1914 p.269.
50. All three groups obtained an extra ½d/hr in 1914 which elevated them from equal lowest in the BoT tables to equal lowest except for Dublin. BoT, *Abstracts*, Vol.17, 1914.
51. Thus at Harmers Clothing, male machine cutters were paid 24/- per week, compared with 26/- to 32/- for craftworkers.
52. Hawkins, *Norwich*, p.51; *Norwich Elector*, 6, (July 1905).
53. *Norwich Elector*, 19, (August 1906). The same article suggested that in retailing generally salesmen aged 20 years or over earned 10/- to 25/- per week, juniors 7/6d to 10/- and porters 18/-. The working week varied between 70 and 90 hours.
54. *Daylight*, 4 May 1901; *Norwich Elector*, 19 (August 1906). Significantly, the ILP urged shopworkers to join the Union of Shop Assistants, Warehousemen and Clerks, but saw their salvation coming via 'their representatives on the floor of the House of Commons'.
55. Hawkins, *Norwich*, p.45 also estimated that men comprised less than 35% of the workers in this sector, excluding brewing, and that women, girls and boys averaged 9/- to 10/- per week.
56. *Norwich Elector*, 15, (April 1906).
57. BoT, *Abstracts*, 10, (1902-4) and 17 (1914).
58. Hawkins, *Norwich*, p.55. BoT, *Abstracts*, 17, (1914).
59. BoT, *Abstracts*, 10 (1902-4) and 17 (1914); Hawkins *Norwich*, p.54.
60. Hawkins, *Norwich*, p.55.
61. BoT, *Abstracts*, 13, (1907-8). In related areas, such as labelling, paper and packaging, there was very little trade union organisation.
62. For example the semi- and unskilled workers on the Council's Direct Works Department were organised, though the establishment of a 21/- minimum wage in this area in 1903 reflects primarily a City Council decision, rather than trade union activity (*Daylight*, 27 June 1903).
63. For the Black Country 'Prairie Fire' strikes in 1913 see M. Haynes, 'The British Working Class in Revolt in 1910-14' *International Socialism*, 2nd series, 22 (1984) pp.87-116. An example in the textile industry is covered in J.L. White, 'Lancashire Cotton Textiles' in Wrigley, ed., *British Industrial Relations*, pp.209-229.
64. In effect, the reverse of the situations examined in R. Challinor, *The Origins of British Bolshevism* (London 1977), Chapter 3, and B. Holton, *British Syndicalism 1900-14* (London 1976), pp.35-8 and see footnote 14 above.
65. This is not to deny that there were class-struggle aspects to electoral contests, but to suggest that these were less open or obvious than in industrial disputes.

Chapter 6

1. See, for example, Bealey and Pelling, *Labour and Politics*.
2. For example, R. McKibben, *The Evolution of the Labour Party 1910-24*, (Oxford 1974) (hereafter McKibben, *Evolution of Labour Party*).
3. See M.Cahill, 'Labour in the Municipalities' in *The First Labour Party 1906-14*, edited by K.D. Brown, (London 1985), pp.89-104.
4. For Morris's warnings on this see Thompson, *William Morris*, esp. pp.542, 621-3 and 800.
5. *Daylight*, 8 September 1900. The ILP Candidate was to have been G.H. Roberts.
6. Roberts, letter to *Daylight*, 27 October 1900. See also NCL, Local Studies Dept., *NMCA* October 1900, *Daylight*, 20 and 27 October 1900.
7. NCL, Local Studies Dept., *NMCA*, October 1900.
8. The Heigham Radical Club opened in 1895 with an initial list of 117 members (*EWL*, 2 February 1895).
9. Thus Norwich SDF campaigned against the Liberal Council which had acquired land upon which to build 'workmen's houses' in 1899 but subsequently failed to make a start. *Norfolk Socialist Review* (hereafter *NSR*) 4, (1901).
10. In Poor Law Guardian Elections, 3 ILP and 1 SDF candidates polled 683 votes altogether.
11. NCL, Local Studies Dept., *NMCA*, October 1902.
12. *EDP* 21 October 1902.
13. *ibid*, 3 November 1903. *Daylight* noted revealingly, 'there is nothing of the fire eater or anarchist

about Mr Witard: he is a well-informed, unassuming man of the better class artisan type . . . he follows the calling of the Industrial Assurance Agent.' (*Daylight*, 28 November 1903).

14. Smith stood as 'Socialist and TU' candidate. see *Daylight*, 10 September 1904
15. F. Henderson, *Citizenship*, 1 (January 1902).
16. Cited by Henderson in Letter to the *Eastern Evening News*, 21 September 1906. (NCL, Local Studies Dept., C.HEN 046, Collection of press cuttings relating to Fred Henderson.
17. *ibid*, February 1903.
18. Cited in *Daylight*, 14 February 1903.
19. This suggests that Liberal commitments to a Norwich 'Progressive Unity' before 1906 were even less than implied in G.L. Bernstein, *Liberalism and Liberal Politics in Edwardian England* (1986) (hereafter Bernstein, *Liberal Politics*).
20. The balance on the City Council since 1900 had been: Liberals 34, Conservatives 30. In 1903 it was Liberals 35, Conservatives 28, Independent Labour Party 1.
21. If there were areas where local Liberal and ILP or LRC organisations willingly co-operated from the outset, Norwich, as will be seen, was not one.
22. The agreement was made on 6 September 1903 and it was further understood that the two parties would 'demonstrate friendliness' to each other in mobilising votes.
23. NCL, Local Studies Dept., TCEC 12 June and 1 August 1900.
24. *ibid*, 12 December 1900; *Daylight*, 23 November 1901.
25. *Daylight*, 22 February 1902.
26. *ibid*, 8 March 1902.
27. *ibid*, 8 February 1902. Burgess's own assessment of Roberts as 'an ambitious windbag' was hardly objective.
28. Thus *Daylight*, could only look forward to the date when 'ILPers, SDFers, Clarionettes, Christian Socialists, Fabians and Radicals will have arrived at the conclusion that there must be some five or six burning issues upon which all might agree.' (*Daylight*, 8 March 1902).
29. Their idea of a Liberal MP was Louis Tillett, the local rising star, solicitor and son of a former Norwich Liberal MP, soon to be the Liberal strategist handling municipal issues.
30. Norwich Liberal Council, 17 September 1902, reported in *Daylight*, 20 September 1902.
31. *EDP* 15 October 1902.
32. *ibid*, 27 December 1902.
33. *ibid*, 7 February 1903.
34. Trade Union branches of the Plumbers, Bricklayers, Carpenters and Joiners, Stonemasons, Plasterers, NUBSO, ASRS, Gasworkers and General, Electricians, Smiths and Fitters all endorsed Roberts, according to *Daylight*, 15 August 1903.
35. *Daylight*, 25 April 1903.
36. This was even though Roberts had entered the field first! *Daylight*, *Election Special*, 20 January 1904. The *EDP* took a similar line.
37. NCL, Local Studies Dept., *NMCA*. Liberal Election Material, January 1904.
38. *Daylight*, 16 January 1904.
39. See Bealey and Pelling *Labour and Politics* p.195.
40. NCL, Local Studies Dept., *NMCA*, January 1904.
41. *EDP*, 18 January 1904. Letter from F. Henderson. Henderson referred retrospectively to the Labour League in another letter to *Daylight*, 4 February 1905. Cf. the treatment of this issue in Bellamy and Saville, *Dictionary of Labour Biography*, (London 1979, 5 vols) *sub* G.H. Roberts, Vol. 4, 149.
42. *Daylight*, 2 December 1905. Letter from F. Henderson.
43. *ibid*, 30 January and 26 March 1904.
44. Norwich Liberal Caucus, meeting, 12 April 1904, reported in *Daylight*, 16 April 1904.
45. *ibid*, same issue.
46. *ibid*, 12 and 26 March 1904. The Norwich ASE branches openly called for an alternative to Roberts as LRC candidate.
47. NCL, Local Studies Dept., *NMCA*, November 1904. H. Rudd, actually a member of the Newsagents Society, defeated J. Gardiner of the ILP in what was acknowledged as a setback for the ILP.
48. See *Daylight* 11 November 1904 and 4 February 1905.
49. The *Norwich Labour Elector* appeared monthly and had an estimated circulation of 5,000. W.R. Smith was appointed Labour Election Agent and Committee Rooms were opened.
50. The Tories' decision to run only one candidate probably reflected their own schisms. Sir Samuel Hoare, the sitting member, was a financier and Free Trade advocate. He either refused to stand alongside, or was replaced by, the Protectionist Ernest Wild, who had already represented the Tories in the 1904 by-election (See *Daylight* 7 May 1904).
51. NCL, Local Studies Dept., *NMCA*, November 1905.
52. *Daylight*, 4 November 1905.
53. Norwich Liberal Executive Committee Statement, 27 November 1905 (cited in *Daylight*, 2 December

117

1905).
54. *EDP*, 8, 9, 14 and 15 December 1905, *sub* 'Local Topics'.
55. *ibid*, 29 December 1905.
56. Labour Election Meeting Report, 3 January (*EDP*, 4 January 1906). Chairing the meeting, W.R. Smith repeatedly asked Labour supporters not to plump for Roberts. Roberts' Election Programme concentrated upon Home Rule, secular education in all state aided schools, provision of school meals, old age pensions and an Eight Hour working day. Only nationalisation of the railways and vague references to 'collective ownership' would have been offputting to most Liberals NCL, Local Studies Dept., *NMCA*, General Election 1906, Labour).
57. *EDP*, 30 December 1905. Report of Liberal Election Meeting on 29 December.
58. Hardie was addressing Labour's Election Rally in St Andrews Hall on 5 January (cited in *Daylight*, 13 January 1906), Henderson's report was printed in the *EDP* 6 January 1906.

Chapter 7

1. Particularly if Labour's vote of 11,072 in 1906 is compared with the ILP vote of 2,444 in the 1904 by-election.
2. For example, R. Douglas, 'Labour in Decline' in *Essays in Anti Labour History*, edited by K.D. Brown (London 1974 (hereafter Brown, *Essays*) pp.105-125. More generally, see W.L. Arnstein, 'Edwardian Politics: Turbulent Spring or Indian Summer?' in *The Edwardian Age*, edited by A. O'Day (London 1979) (hereafter O'Day, *Edwardian Age*) pp.60-78.
3. The ILP in Norwich claimed that it was the subject of a Liberal/Tory alliance from 1908 onwards. The Conservative group controlled the City Council from 1907 onwards.
4. See for example J. Hinton, 'The Rise of a Mass Labour Movement: Growth and Limits' in Wrigley, *British Industrial Relations*, pp.20-46, and B. Holton, *British Syndicalism 1900-1914* (London 1976), pp.35-8.
5. *Norwich Elector*, 19 (July 1906). Between four and six street-meetings continued to be held weekly.
6. Information from NCL, Local Studies Dept., *NMCA*, *Daylight* and *EDP*. The table refers only to ILP gains or losses of seats and includes municipal by-elections. Details as to candidacies, votes etc are given in the text below.
7. NCL, Local Studies Dept., *NMCA*, 1906-13.
8. *ibid*, 1905, 1906. The total ILP vote was 1,617 compared with the 960 votes cast for three ILP candidates in 1905.
9. *EDP*, 21 September 1906. Letter from F. Henderson.
10. *ibid* and *Daylight*, 29 September. Many ILP members assessed Henderson as 'a Wobbler'. This underestimated his own self-interest while nicely summarising his political position.
11. NCL, Local Studies Dept., *NMCA*, 1906.
12. *EDP*, 2 November 1906 and *Daylight*, 10 November 1906.
13. An early issue clearly expresses the SDF's electoral emphasis: 'in place of the hideous strike weapon of the trade unionist . . . the use of the ballot box should be substituted, used in an organised manner, with a view to destroying all class distinctions and privileges'. (*NSR*, 3, 1901 12-3).
14. Thus from July to September 1905 the ILP held 23 open air meetings, the SDF 21 (*Norwich Elector*, 6, July 1905). Of course, this says nothing of attendances.
15. *Daylight*, 11 November 1905.
16. NCL, Local Studies Dept., *TCEC*, 31 January and 18 February 1907; *Daylight*, 30 March 1907. Three of the ILP members were elected in Mousehold ward.
17. NCL, Local Studies Dept., *ibid*, 18 July and 2 September 1907.
18. The election respectively of an ILP member and the Socialist Victor Grayson in these constituencies was noted in *Daylight*, 27 July 1907. In Liverpool Kirkdale the ILP was exposed to the playing of the 'Orange card'. See, for example, Howell, *British Workers*, p.206.
19. These included the Rev. Cummings, ILP Guardian elected in Catton Ward in 1905, and the Rev. Campbell, Founder of the Norwich Labour Church and author of innumerable letters to the press on the theme 'Socialism is the pure and undefiled religion of Jesus Christ'. See *Norwich Elector*, 23 (December 1906) and *Daylight*, 12 October 1907.
20. NCL, Local Studies Dept., *NMCA*, 1907, Conservatives. 'No surrender to Socialists' was another slogan on the standard leaflet.
21. *ibid*, Conservative leaflet in Catton ward where Bunting was the Tory candidate.
22. Two other ILP candidates, Savage (a shoemaker) in Fye Bridge and Manning (a compositor) in Wensum both failed, as did A. Segon of the SDF in Heigham Ward.
23. The ILP lost a seat to the Conservatives in Coslany, where the Tory's victory was the first there for ten years.
24. *Daylight*, 9 November 1907.
25. *ibid*, 16 November 1907.

26. The SDF retained, formally at least, the politics of class struggle and a scepticism of the role of the capitalist State, both of which were lacking in the socialism of the ILP.

27. *Daylight*, 30 May 1908.

28. These were in Fye Bridge, Heigham, Catton and Mousehold wards. Total ILP vote was 2,492, an average per candidate of 498.

29. *EDP*, 3 November 1908. 22 people had joined the ILP in the Catton Ward contest.

30. *Daylight*, 27 February and 20 March 1909. The ILP had been further strengthened by the return of H.E. Witard (its first Norwich councillor and former President) from London to take up the post of full-time Organiser in May 1908.

31. NCL, Local Studies Dept., *NMCA*, 1909. Total ILP vote was 2,861, an average per candidate of 572. Only in Fye Bridge ward did the ILP record a smaller vote than in 1908.

32. *ibid*, 1910. This allegation was made in ILP Municipal leaflets in the contest of 1910.

33. *ibid*, 1910, ILP.

34. See R. Douglas 'Labour in Decline' in Brown *Essays*, and M.G. Sheppard and J.L. Halstead, 'Labour's Municipal Performance in Provincial England and Wales 1901-13', in *Society for the Study of Labour History Bulletin*, 39, (Autumn 1979).

35. 'Containment' of the Socialist element within ILP politics remained, for this was the direction taken by ILP leaders since its founding conference, viz, an emphasis upon Parliamentary influence and a willingness to do whatever necessary to obtain this.

36. 'Enfranchised population' is a very poor substitute for the Labour Movement particularly when 40% of all males (almost all of these likely to have been working class) and all women were not enfranchised.

37. *Daylight*, 20 March, 3 April and 5 June 1909.

38. *ibid*, 15 May 1909. The second Tory candidate was H. Snowden.

39. See W.L. Arnstein 'Edwardian Politics . . .' in O'Day *The Edwardian Age*.

40. As reported in *Daylight*, 4 July 1908 and 23 January 1909.

41. Roberts, Labour Election Meeting, 5 January, (*EDP*, 6 January 1910).

42. Low, Liberal Election Meeting, 6 January, (*EDP*, 7 January 1910).

43. A vote in a double seat constituency is not directly comparable with overall national results, but may indicate a deviation in Norwich from national patterns: viz, Labour and Liberal vote in Norwich 58%, Nationally 51%. Conservative vote in Norwich 42%, Nationally 47%.

44. 10,679 people voted for Low and Roberts, with just 206 Labour and 325 Liberal Plumpers. 7,842 voted for both the Conservative candidates.

45. See O'Day, *The Edwardian Age*, pp.75-6.

46. NCL, Local Studies Dept., *NMCA*, W. Dyson, 'Address to the Electors of Norwich', December 1910, Conservative. The Osborne judgement blocked the use of general trade union funds for Labour Party purposes.

47. *ibid*. Along with Tariff reform 'an efficient army and a supreme navy' Dyson advocated Votes for Women on the current conditions and qualifications pertaining to men, and Poor Law Reform 'to abolish the stigma which too often attaches to the receipt of Poor Law Relief today'.

48. Report on Liberal Adoption Meeting (*EDP*, 25 November 1910).

49. NCL, Local Studies Dept., *NMCA* G.H. Roberts, 'Election Address', December 1910, Labour.

50. 9,279 people voted for Low and Roberts while 650 voters plumped for the Liberal and 529 for Labour. Only 229 voted for Dyson and Low, and just 209 for Dyson and Roberts (*EDP* 6 December 1910).

51. W.R. Smith and G.H. Roberts (cited in *EDP*, 6 December 1910). Ironically, Smith would be one of the Labour candidates who would dislodge the turn-coat Tory Roberts in 1923/4.

52. Since 1908 the shoe industry agreement had meant neither strikes nor wage claims in the local industry.

53. Thus W.R. Smith, the S.D.F. member, strike leader and President of Norwich NUBSO in 1897 was in 1910 still a NUBSO and Trades Council official, but also an ILP City Councillor, Election Agent and Justice of the Peace.

54. In January 1911.

55. A point stressed from the Liberal Party perspective in Bernstein, *Liberal Politics*, p.117.

Chapter 8

1. Without evidence on Party social composition information on candidates has to suffice. See McKibbin, *Evolution of Labour Party*, 1974, *Introduction*, p.xiii; Bernstein, *Liberal Politics*, p.201.

2. See G. Foote, *The Labour Party's Political Thought* (London 1986), pp.19-37.

3. See, for example, E.J. Hobsbawm, 'Trends in the British Labour Movement since 1850' in *Labouring Men*, edited by E.J. Hobsbawm, (London 1964) pp.316-343; D. Dean, 'The Character of the Early Labour Party in O'Day *Edwardian Age*, pp.97-112.

4. *Daylight*, 24 January 1891.

5. *ibid*, 6 December 1902, 19 December 1903, 10 December 1904, *EDP*, 5 December 1905.

6. NCL, Local Studies Dept., *TCEC*, 2 October 1905.
7. *Daylight*, 3 March 1906, 9 March 1907.
8. *ibid*, 23 March 1909. See also R.H. Mottram, *Success to the Mayor; the development of Local Government in Norwich*, (London 1937), p.263.
9. *Daylight*, 27 June 1903. This achievement was claimed by the ILP as their own in 'The ILP on the City Council' (by H.E. Witard) in *ILP 23rd Annual Conference Souvenir*, (Norwich 1915).
10. These arrangements were extended to the City Engineers and Sanitary Departments (*Norwich Elector*, 3, April 1905).
11. *EDP*, 16 June 1909.
12. *Daylight*, 17 and 24 February 1900.
13. *Norwich Elector*, 7, (August 1905); *Daylight*, 9 September 1905.
14. The cost of meals for other children was 1d for breakfast and 1½d for dinner (*Daylight*, 16 February and 15 June 1907).
15. *EDP*, 16 December 1908. Report of the Council Meeting.
16. *ibid*, 16 June 1909.
17. J. Whitely, Social Investigations and the Poor Law in Norwich 1906-14, (hereafter 'Social Investigations') (Unpublished MA Dissertation, University of East Anglia 1968), p.15.
18. *Daylight*, 30 March 1907; J. Stackhouse, 'Changes in the Administration of the Poor Law in Norwich 1871-1908' (unpublished MA Dissertation, University of East Anglia, 1971), pp.40-41.
19. *Daylight*, 10 September 1904.
20. Evidence to the Poor Law Commissioners by Captain Hervey, 1909, Cmd 4626, Appendix Vol.1A.
21. Causing a split among the Liberal Guardians in the process.
22. Committee of Investigators, *The Destitute of Norwich and how they live* (Norwich 1912), pp.13-16. The methodology of the Committee was endorsed by Seebohm Rowntree, who prefaced the 2nd and 3rd editions of the Report after the majority of the Guardians had tried to refute it.
23. *ibid*, pp.16-17, 34-35, 60.
24. Whitely, 'Social Investigations' p.141.
25. A notable absentee from the Minority's supporters was G.H. Roberts MP.
26. cf. G.L. Bernstein, 'Liberalism' 617-640 which seems too influenced by the paper proposals of the Liberal Municipal Reform Programme, the work of Henderson.
27. Interpretations stressing 'economic class solidarity' in Labour's rise include D.E. Martin, 'The Instruments of the People?' in *Ideology and the Labour Movement*, edited by D.E. Martin and D. Rubinstein (London 1979), pp.125-146, R. McKibbin, *Evolution of Labour Party*.
28. NCL, Local Studies Dept., *NMCA*, 1911.
29. Labour's average vote, 497, was marginally down on previous years.
30. NCL, Local Studies Dept., *NMCA*, 1912. The average Labour vote was now 719.
31. *EDP*, 3 November 1913.
32. Bernstein 'Liberalism', p.624, Table 1.
33. Material cited is drawn from *NMCA*. 21 people were involved in the 46 candidacies.
34. Of the remaining six instances, on three occasions the candidate was a member of the SDF and there were solitary 'Socialist/Trade Union', 'Socialist' and 'Municipal Reform Union' candidates.
35. The two were Municipal Reform Union candidates. See ch.6 above.
36. Thus while F. Easton (ILP) owned two newsagents shops, A Segon (SDF) was definitely 'getting by' as best he could.
37. In working class wards: of the 46 candidacies, 41 were in workers' residential or industrial areas: Coslany, Catton, Wensum, Mousehold, Heigham or Fye Bridge.
38. Though these dated from the middle 1880 and 1890s and do not seem to have expanded in the Edwardian years.
39. Thus the Liberal Trade Unionist Scott was a delegate to the MRU and one of its municipal candidates.
40. Excludes municipal by-elections, and cases where candidate withdrew before polling day.
41. *Daylight*, 8 October 1898.
42. Bernstein, *Liberal Politics*, rather neglects 'working-men liberals' and sees the Party's rank and file as almost exclusively middle class.
43. *ibid*, p.24.
44. *ibid*, p.200.
45. In their different ways G. Dangerfield, *The Strange Death of Liberal England* (London 1935), and Pelling, *Origins of Labour Party*, convey the inevitability of their subject's respective fate.
46. See R. Dowse, *Left in the Centre: The ILP 1893-1940*, (London 1966), (hereafter Dowse, *ILP*) p.19.
47. The three ILP councillors in 1907 comprised a warehouseman, insurance agent and political agent; in 1910, an insurance agent, political agent and a journalist; in 1913, insurance supervisor, political agent, journalist, two shoeworkers and one 'other'. The ILP had its 'industrial' activists but the issue here is who played the leading political roles. The work of the Political Agent was essentially geared to the Electoral Register, canvassing etc. and probably to monitoring trade union work, rather than

co-ordinating shopfloor activities.

Chapter 9

1. Allowing for different perceptions of class interest on the part of, say, a Liberal-voting craft trade unionist, compared with a revolutionary socialist shoeworker in the SL.
2. See above, Chapter 3, pp.32-3.
3. See eg. Clegg, Fox and Thompson, *British Trade Unions*, pp.78-85 for a brief summary.
4. See above, Chapter 1 p.10, and Chapter 3 pp.28-30.
5. Cited in Groves, *Sickle*, p.105. Pelling, *Origins of Labour Party*, p.198 also stresses the links between socialists and the shoe industry in Norwich and Leicester. But in 1903 no less then 19,500 trade unionists, including 13,000 NUBSO members, were affiliated to the Leicester Trades Council, (Howell, *British Workers*, p.231). Comparative figures for Norwich were 1,200 and nearly 400. The maximum number of NUBSO members in Norwich in 1908 was roughly 3,100, (Fox, *History of NUBSO* , p.316.
6. In conditions of 'war work', the number of trade unionists affiliated to the Norwich Trades Council was estimated at 9,000 (*ILP 23rd Annual Conference Souvenir*, Norwich 1915).
7. Howell has noted this pattern in areas of trade union weakness such as the West Yorkshire woollen centres, though the behaviour of the 'Millocracy' there was not paralleled in Norwich (Howell, *British Workers*, p.277-8).
8. See J. Hinton, *Labour and Socialism* (Brighton 1983), pp.62-3 for an exposition of this argument.
9. See above, Chapter 5 p.58-9, and P. Bagwell, *The Railwaymen*, (London 1963), pp.234-5. As for NUBSO, the main Norwich No.1 branch was neither affiliated to the local Trades Council nor the LRC as late as February 1905 (*Daylight*, 4 February 1905).
10. See above, Chapter 1 p.15.
11. A. Howkins, 'Edwardian Liberalism and Industrial Unrest: A Class View of the Decline of Liberalism', *History Workshop Journal*, 4, (Autumn 1977), 148.
12. Howkins generalises too much from St Faiths but his point that models of a recovering New Liberalism (eg Clarke, *Lancashire*) do not cover the Norfolk experience and may not necessarily be all that general, seems valid.
13. Compare this with West Yorkshire, (K. Laybourn and J. Reynolds, *Liberalism and the Rise of Labour 1880-1918*, (1984) (hereafter *Rise of Labour*)). For Wales, see K.O. Morgan, 'The New Liberalism and the Challenge of Labour: the Welsh Experience 1885-1929', in Brown (ed.)*Essays*, esp. p.164.
14. McKibbin notes that: 'however much the Liberal and Labour Parties had in common politically, socially they were a world apart'. This of itself did not guarantee the course or form of future political changes however. McKibbin, *Evolution of Labour Party*, Introduction p.xviii.
15. Again, such progress was far from the linear, almost inevitable, path suggested by Pelling in his *Origins of Labour Party*.
16. Laybourn and Reynolds noted that in West Yorkshire, weak unions were 'ignored when they demanded political concessions from other parties; but the way lay open for the creation of an independent working class party.' (Laybourn and Reynolds, *Rise of Labour*, pp.27-8.)
17. An argument which in any case ignores 'Labour' in the sense of the Labour and Trade Union movement. See P.F. Clarke, *Lancashire*, p.406.
18. See C. Cook, 'Labour and the Downfall of the Liberal Party 1906-14', in *Crisis and Controversy: Essays in Honour of A.J.P. Taylor*, edited by A. Sked and C. Cook, (London 1976), pp.38-65.
19. Viz Free Trade, Reform of the House of Lords.
20. In this respect it could be argued that Labour was restraining itself. See, for example, Howell, *British Workers*, pp.20-1, and McKibbin *Evolution of Labour Party*, p.48.
21. G.H. Roberts, the MP, is one case in point. Another was F. Henderson, 'dealing' with the Liberals in all manner of behind-the-scenes work long after he joined the ILP. See, for example, letter from P.F. Pollard ILP Eastern Divisional Secretary, dated 13 December 1914 in J.F. Henderson, Correspondence, HEN 15/5 383x7, Norfolk County Record Office.
22. Though this is not to say that ideas are totally independent or that 'consciousness determines being'.
23. cf. Pelling, *Origins of Labour Party*, p.218 and Groves *Sickle*, pp.98-9
24. '... lacking as it did any real theoretical basis it could accommodate practically anything a trade unionist was likely to demand' (Dowse, *ILP*, p.3).
25. Howell, *British Workers*, p.10.
26. The Norwich Labour Church was founded in January 1907, the first socialist holiday camp at nearby Caister in 1906.
27. See Dowse, *ILP*, p.18 and Tsuzuki, *Hyndman*, pp.174-5.
28. As argued, for example, by D.E. Martin, 'The Instruments of the People?' in *Ideology and the Labour Movement*, edited by D.E. Martin and O. Rubinstein (London 1979), pp.125-146.

121

Index

Where possible information on local individuals is included (eg. SOC, TU, Lib etc). This relates to their activity in the years up to 1914 only.